EXPLORE THE MYSTERIES OF SACRED SEXUALITY

"We are not only physical beings on a spiritual path, but spiritual beings on a physical path."

—Bonnie Johnston and Peter Schuerman

Experience the transformative effect of sexual magick. Discover exhilarating sexual techniques to liberate your consciousness from cultural conditioning. *Sex, Magick & Spirit* presents a positive, intimate approach to the often repressed power of human sexuality.

Sex, Magick & Spirit is the first book to openly discuss the Sexual Mysteries of the West in a way that is relevant to modern times. Here is a fascinating account of the origin of the Mysteries which have influenced our culture from Paleolithic times to the present day. The Mysteries cannot be explained; they must be experienced to be fully understood. No one can teach the Mysteries, they can only guide you through magical techniques that can allow you to tap in to higher states of consciousness.

Arouse the power deep within yourself and create a unique connection to the Divine. Create balanced gender roles and healthy relationships based upon love and mutual respect. Learn a positive and fulfilling approach to personal transformation. *Sex, Magick & Spirit* takes sex to the next level.

Throughout history, people have utilized the energies of sexual union in ritualized ways, such as the Sacred Marriage, the Great Rite of Wicca, or Thelemic sex magick. Today, you are encouraged to explore sacred sexuality in a magickal context by designing your own sensually satisfying rituals. *Sex, Magick & Spirit* provides numerous exercises and special techniques for enhancing and exploring the sexual experience, for either one person or a couple. Learn how to use sensuality and intimacy to reclaim sex as a spiritual act of love and pleasure.

ABOUT THE AUTHORS

Bonnie Johnston is a mythologist who seeks to revive the mysteries of the ancient world in a way that suits the modern mind. She holds a B.A. in English from the University of California at Davis. Her interests include ancient history, poetry, trance channeling, divination, martial arts, ritualism, tantric witchcraft, and the creation of magickal tools. She is the author of *Sibyl*, a goddess-based divination system.

Peter Schuerman is a pagan philosopher and biologist whose interests include divination, transpersonal consciousness, sex magick, tantra, information theory, linguistics, shamanism, and playing the *didjeridu,* and Australian aboriginal instrument. He holds a B.S. in botany and a Ph.D. in genetics, and has extensively studied the patterns of evolution that cultural and biological systems share.

Johnston and Schuerman are the co-creators of *The Elysian Oracle,* a divination system based on the cosmology of the ancient Greeks.

ENLIGHTENMENT
THROUGH ECSTASY

SEX,
MAGICK,
AND
SPIRIT

BONNIE L. JOHNSTON
PETER L. SCHUERMAN

1998
Llewellyn Publications
St. Paul, Minnesota 55164-0383, U.S.A.

FIRST EDITION
First Printing, 1998
Cover design by Tom Grewe
Cover photo by Christopher Grajczk
Editing and book design by Ken Schubert

Library of Congress Cataloging-in-Publication Data
Johnston, Bonnie L., 1968–
    Sex, magick, and spirit : enlightenment through ecstacy / Bonnie
  L. Johnston, Peter L. Schuerman. -- 1st ed.
      p. cm.
    Includes bibliographical references and index.
    ISBN 1–56718–378–6 (pbk.)
    1. Sex--Religious aspects. 2. Magic. I. Schuerman, Peter L. ,
  1965–   . II. Title.
BL65.S4J64   1997
291.2'12--dc21   97–39122
                                             CIP

Llewellyn Publications
A Division of Llewellyn Worldwide, Ltd.
P.O. 64383, Dept. K378-6 St. Paul, MN 55164-0383

Printed in the United States of America

Table of Contents

Illustration Credits

All original illustrations in Chapters Four through Nine and on chapter title pages by Carrie Westfall.

All other illustrations not listed below courtesy of Dover Publications.

Page 14 From a nineteenth-century engraving of Carravagio's *Psyche Received into Olympus.*

Page 18 Photographs of statues of Gaia and Willendorf Goddess by Oberon Zell and Morning Glory Zell, used courtesy of of Mythic Images, P.O. Box 1775, Laytonville, CA 95454. (707) 984-0024.

Page 20 Illustration of Sin from *Sur le Cult de Mithra,* 1847.

Page 29 From Jost Amman's *Kunstbüchlin,* printed by Johann Fayerabend, Frankfurt, 1599.

Page 31 Photograph labeled "Hellenic Artemis:" Silver Greek coin (12 Litrae), late third century, from Syracuse, Sicily. From the Michael A. Sikora collection. Used by permission.

Page 35 Illustration of Ishtar by Alexandra Lumen, Llewellyn.

Page 45 Photograph of a sculpture of Pan by Henry A. Pegram from *Classic Myth and Legend,* Gresham Publishing Company (n.d.)

Page 49 Illustration of Tammuz by Lisa Novak, Llewellyn.

Preface

This book is about the Sexual Mysteries of Western culture, and is based on experiences we have had while studying both Eastern Tantra and Western sex magic, and on our research into the history and mythology of various ancient cultures. You do not need to study Eastern philosophy or religious thought to practice the exercises described in this book. It will not be necessary for you to re-create the lifestyle of an ancient Japanese sage or Buddhist monk. Our exercises are designed for Westerners who wish to explore the sacred sexual heritage of the Western world, in the Western world. This book is not about traditional Eastern Tantra.

This book is not a sex manual—there are already a plethora of "how to be a better lover" books available. We are not concerned with sexual technique but with the use of the physical body as a means of exploring consciousness. However, if the idea of trying things like oral sex or "exotic" sexual positions bothers you, you are reading the wrong book.

This book is also not for people who label sex as "spiritual" only because it helps them come to terms with their repressed physical urges.

We have chosen to focus on some of the more advanced and esoteric aspects of sex. Some authors, when writing about sexuality, discuss the importance of loving the self as the foundation for loving others, make a case for sex being natural and healthy, concentrate on relaxing sexual anxieties, and provide exercises that encourage partners to respect each other. While these are worthy teachings, the discussion in this book is for students who no longer need to be convinced of these basic principles, and who wish to go a step beyond. In taking this next step, we leave behind the efforts to make sex secure and comfortable, and enter a realm in which sex is used to question the very nature of our being. This type of introspection can be, by turns, both disturbing and exhilarating.

The Sexual Mysteries of ancient cultures dealt with the relationship between men and women. As this book is based on these mysteries, lesbians and gay men may feel left out of the discussion. However, this need not be the case. Homosexual couples can make use of these exercises and apply these philosophies just as well as heterosexuals. As we will see, a key concept in the Sexual Mysteries is the generation of polarity at various levels of being, and the subsequent synthesis of these polarities. The Sexual Mysteries can work for any couple open-minded enough to try them. However, because of our reliance on mythological sources for this book (which are primarily heterosexual in nature), many of the examples may have to be adapted slightly for homosexual couples.

As a final note, we'd like to point out that, while the Sexual Mysteries are not "safe," it is important to be safe about sex itself. Your body is literally the temple in which the Sexual Mysteries will be explored. Respect it, protect it, and it will teach you things you cannot now imagine.

Live, love and learn,
Peter Schuerman
Bonnie Johnston
Summer 1996

ONE

The Sexual Mysteries

S ex is a potent method of directing and releasing magical energies. The sexual act unites the polarities that exist within us, creating a strong current of energy which can be used to transform consciousness. This transformation of consciousness is the truest goal of magic; sex can literally be a magical experience. Sex can be used to transform human consciousness because the sexual act is a gateway to divine consciousness.

Using sex for personal transformation can be difficult: even if you sincerely believe that sex is sacred, you may be confused about how to proceed. At the moment, there is a great interest in the Eastern tradition called Tantra. Tantra is a system of sacred sexuality which was formed in India and carried to China and Japan thousands of years ago. It is only within the last hundred years or so that the teachings of Tantra have filtered into the Western world, and many of these teachings have been watered down or oversimplified for those unfamiliar with esoteric Eastern religious beliefs. Unfortunately, the teachings of Tantra also incorporate a number of cultural biases, adopted from the cultures in which Tantra developed. These cultural biases make understanding the principles of sacred sex more difficult for Western students.

TANTRA

Tantric philosophy arose and developed in the context of the ancient East. It can be very frustrating to translate the information contained in Tantric texts into a form that is compatible with a modern Western lifestyle, especially one in which men and women are considered equals. Delving into these ancient materials and attempting to separate spiritual truth from cultural bias can be tedious. Some Tantric teachings foster the idea that the sexual act is a form of competition, in which the man and the woman try to steal sexual energies or precious fluids from each other (see Chapter Five). This is a result of the fact that the social role of women was extremely limited at the time Tantric practice was solidified. The study of Tantra by modern Westerners is made more difficult because many of the ancient Tantric writers were not seeking understanding or enlightenment, but were searching for a path to physical immortality.

SEX MAGIC AND PAGANISM

Although many magical and pagan groups include sexuality in their rituals, they often do so for the wrong reasons. Very few truly understand the transformative power of sex, and instead use it as a form of religious celebration. This is certainly not a bad use, but it does not recognize the full potential of sacred sex. Using sexual ritual as a way to rebel against our society's general disapproval of sex can have positive effects on the psyche—but again, this is a fairly limited use which does not take advantage of the true power of sexuality as a tool for change.

Unfortunately, there are those who would abuse sexual rites for their own purposes, using these practices as an excuse to be promiscuous or as an attempt to have sex without commitment. At worst, sex is included in rituals for its shock value, or made into a religious duty. Any group that asks you to demonstrate your faith or devotion by having sex with another member of that group should be avoided. Sex can be initiatory, but it should never be obligatory.

SACRED SEXUALITY

In order to recognize the sacred nature of sex, you must first be willing to recognize the sacred nature of your partner, and your partner must be willing to see the divine in you. Neither person should be treated as a resource to be exploited, or as a stepping stone to another level of consciousness. Respect for the divine implies a respect for every individual, because each of us contains the divine within, and each of us makes up a small part of divinity.

Sacred sex is a celebration of many things, but it is not merely celebratory. It is also a means of practicing magic, of transforming your consciousness in positive ways. You do not need to join a group or a religion to experience it, and you do not need to devote your life to a guru to find it. You do not need to live in a monastery to meditate on it. You can practice it with your current partner (or partners) in your own bedroom or kitchen, or minivan, or treehouse, etc.

Ancient peoples used sex as a transformative force for thousands of years. These practices arose in the cultures that gave rise to Western civilization, and they formed around a pattern of gender roles which is still prevalent even today. These roles create polarities which, when brought together, result in the transformation of consciousness. These practices comprised the Western approach to transformation of consciousness through sexuality, just as Tantra was the Eastern approach.

The Sexual Mysteries existed in Egypt, in the Semitic cultures of the Near East, and in ancient Greece. It is interesting to note that as each of these cultures became increasingly more urban and lost their connections with nature, they also lost these mysteries. To revive the Sexual Mysteries, we will need an understanding of humankind's relationship to nature, a desire to connect with divinity, and a healthy attitude toward sexuality.

THE ANCIENT ROOTS OF SACRED SEXUALITY IN THE WEST

It would be a mistake for us to try to literally re-create the details of ancient life. Our romanticization of the ancient world often fools us into thinking that life was ideal for our ancestors, when in fact, they faced the same types of problems that we do—disease, poverty, war, and, of course, domestic difficulties. In addition, ancient people lacked many of the things that our technology makes possible, things we would probably miss if we were suddenly deprived of them. A steady supply of safe food and clean water, worldwide communication and travel, computers, movies, television and books are all benefits of living with modern technology. We would be foolish to indiscriminately discard our own culture, with its good and bad elements, for another culture's good and bad elements.

However, we can see from mythology and historical accounts that there were periods when ancient peoples had something we lack—a deep sense of the divinity that manifests when two people join in love. In order to taste this, we need to understand the Sexual Mysteries and find a way to adapt them to the modern world, as opposed to simply re-creating the details of the mysteries and hoping that understanding will follow.

We will focus on the Sexual Mysteries of ancient Greece, ancient Egypt, and the Near East. Each of these cultures has made significant contributions to modern Western culture, and each possessed the Sexual Mysteries at the time when settled agricultural communities and nomadic herding tribes were joining to create the earliest civilizations, which manifested as urban societies.

Settled agricultural communities and nomadic hunter-herder tribes have very different forms of consciousness, and they relate to the world in very different ways. Urban societies, which arise from the joining of these two types of culture, have a hybrid consciousness very similar to our own. We are settled like agrarians. Although few of us cultivate our own food, most of us have permanent addresses. At the same time, we also possess a mobility that is similar to that of nomadic cultures: we "hunt and gather" food from stores, many of us travel regularly to see family or to vacation, and many of us migrate for career purposes or other perceived advantages a number of times during our lives.

The key to applying the wisdom of ancient cultures is to understand that we do not need to adopt the outer forms of their lives. We don't need to give up the things we have achieved, and we don't have to plow fields, spin thread, or hunt game (although we can experience these activities if we choose). Primitive conditions are not a requirement for understanding the spirituality of ancient peoples. What we must do is live like them in an inner way. We need to understand the principles underlying the Sexual Mysteries, and apply those principles to our own lives. We need to be aware of the influence of the gods in our everyday lives, to see each other as reflections of divinity, and to see ourselves as a part of nature. It is within the framework of these beliefs that the sacred nature of sex becomes apparent.

This level of consciousness is available to everyone. We cannot tell you what this consciousness is, but we can tell you how to find it, so that you can experience it for yourself.

TWO

Mysteries and the Nature of Consciousness

Mysteries are things that cannot be explained in words, but must be experienced in order to be understood. Love is a mystery: you never really understand what all the fuss is about until it happens to you. Parenthood is a mystery: although others may describe it to you, their descriptions cannot really communicate the actual experience of bringing another life into the world. Sex is a mystery: it has the potential to produce changes in consciousness that cannot be made through logical analysis. (Mysteries are different than secrets—a mystery is a thing that cannot be understood through mere explanation; a secret is something that someone else is merely unwilling to share.)

Although mysteries cannot be explained, the techniques for tapping into these mysteries can be. However, these techniques should never be confused with the mysteries themselves. It is possible to master the technique and still fail to understand the mysteries. It is important that you realize no one can teach the mysteries—they can only guide you toward them.

Mystery techniques have the effect of altering your consciousness so as to allow you to tap into information and ways of thinking that you cannot access in you normal state of consciousness. How do these techniques work? Where does this information come from? For answers, we need to look at how the mind works.

CONSCIOUSNESS

What is the mind? Modern models of consciousness argue that mind is a result of activity within the brain. In this materialist model, each person has their own separate consciousness, and each person's thoughts are stored, in physical form, somewhere in their brain.

This model doesn't work. It doesn't allow for magical experiences such as telepathy, precognition, past-life recall, channeling, and communication with deities. The faithful materialist is forced to reject the idea of magic, and to see these "unexplainable" phenomena as illusory.

Many people who have been indoctrinated into the materialist way of thinking try to reconcile their mystical experiences with materialism. As a result, perfectly valid spiritual insights are translated into pseudo-scientific gobbledygook. Rather than allowing a spiritual truth to stand on its own, they feel the need to apologize for its lack of scientific verifiability, and end up looking even flakier than they would have if they'd stuck to what they'd learned. And so we have people trying to explain how thoughts "radiate" from the brain to create telepathy, how deities are really just psychological constructs, how the collective unconscious is really encoded into your DNA, and how channelers are merely tapping into "unused" parts of their brains.

Forget all of that. You are always using all of your brain, just as you are always using all of any living organ in your body—the fact that science hasn't figured out *how* you are using it is irrelevant. Your brain is not "beaming messages" to anyone. Deities are real and alive, regardless of how safe it makes people feel to think of them as psychological constructs. DNA encodes biological information, not folklore. These pseudo-scientific explanations are the result of spiritualists who feel the need to apologize to science for experiencing things that science cannot yet explain. They are not comfortable with the idea that a phenomenon could be real and still not be accounted for by current scientific theory.

The fact that science has not caught up yet with human spirituality does not invalidate the existence of the latter. Science has its own areas of expertise, and at the moment, mysticism is not one of them. Does this mean we should give up trying to figure out how these unexplained phenomena work? Of course not—but we should be very careful to remember not to confuse the physical analogies we create with what is actually happening. An analogy is a model for a given situation, it is not an "explanation" of that situation.

MAGICAL CONSCIOUSNESS

The basic idea behind magical or mystical consciousness is connection. This theme appears over and over again in mystical teachings. We are all connected. All is one. The gods dwell within us, and we dwell within the gods.

Consciousness is a continuum, a great pool in which we store our memories, and from which we can draw information. Where is it? This question is meaningless, for consciousness is a part of space-time, but it is not a "thing" in the physical sense. We know it exists, not because we have seen it, but because we observe its effects. An analogy for this is magnetism. We cannot directly observe it, because it is invisible and intangible. However, we can observe a magnet's effect on iron filings. The effects of consciousness, however, cannot be seen by observing the inanimate. They are made most apparent by observation of living creatures, and especially by observation of our selves. The intangible quality of consciousness can be difficult to think about, and we need a conceptual model that fits our understanding. Because we exist in space-time, a space-time model is easiest for us to grasp.

For instance, imagine that every day you write about your experiences in a journal. Imagine a huge, labyrinthine library that everyone has access to. In that library, there is a shelf where you keep your journals. Everyone else is doing the same thing, and any of us can check out any book we can find.

Unfortunately for us, there is no librarian and no card catalog listing the contents of the library. Finding a specific book can be extremely frustrating. So most of the time we stick to our own books, because they are most relevant to us and are the easiest to find. Sometimes, however, we stumble across someone else's shelf and find something interesting.

If you prefer a more modern model, consider the Internet. You keep your own files in your own directory, and only you have access to them. Everyone else keeps their files in their own directories—if everyone stored their files in the same directory, it'd be nearly impossible to find yours when you needed them. However, there are ways of accessing other people's files—by borrowing or "hacking" their password, for instance.

Using these analogies, telepathy is reading someone else's journal or someone else's files. Past-life recall is dusting off an old book, or finding a long-forgotten file. Precognition? Here the above analogies must be modified slightly. The fact that instances of "future memory" do occur[1] suggests that it is possible to borrow a book that has not yet been written in our time, or rather, to move your attention forward in consciousness to the future, in much the same way that we remember the past by moving our attention backwards in consciousness and time.

These models are consistent with most spiritual teachings and with the mystical experiences of many people. Further proof of this model comes from experiments done by transpersonal psychologists such as Stanislav Grof. His book, *The Holotropic Mind,* is an excellent resource for exploring this model of consciousness. Dr. Grof states:

> . . . *[M]ental functions are linked to biological processes in our brains. However, this does not necessarily mean that consciousness originates in or is produced by our brains. This conclusion made by Western science is a metaphysical assumption rather than a scientific fact, and it is certainly possible to come up with other interpretations of the same data. To draw an analogy: A good television repair person can look at the particular distortion of the picture or sound of a television set and tell us exactly what is wrong with it and which parts must be replaced to make the set work properly again. No one would see this as proof that the set itself was responsible for the programs we see when we turn it on. Yet, this is precisely the kind of argument mechanistic science offers for "proof" that consciousness is produced by the brain.*[2]

Consciousness moves in and out of us all the time, like air. We absorb it, process it, and re-emit it. With every thought, the consciousness field that we are embedded in evolves and changes. A great deal occurs in the field of consciousness that we are not aware of. We each tend to tune in to a small portion of the available field, and for good reason. Tuning in too much information is confusing and can make retaining your sense of identity difficult. Techniques for altering consciousness allow you to tune into different aspects of the field, or tune in more than one "wavelength" at a time.[3] Since memories are not actually contained in the brain, it is not impossible for you to "remember" someone else's memories, if you are able to tune into the right wavelength. Certain people are much better at this than others, and we often regard them as mind-readers or psychics.

The Nature of Deities

Popular science fiction often explores the idea that vast artificial intelligences may someday be created by linking a large number of computers together under the right circumstances. In fact, this has already happened—but not with computers.

Consciousness is a field that connects us all, and deities are the vast intelligences made possible by that interconnectivity. They are intelligences that live within us, and that we live within. A deity is a transcendent collection of living consciousness, and living creatures such as ourselves are, conversely, individualized portions of divine consciousness. One analogy for our relationship with the divine would be the relationship of a cell to the body in which it resides. Another analogy for divine consciousness is holographic: divine consciousness is a hologram, and we are each a fragment of that hologram. Each fragment of a hologram contains the entire image carried by the original, except that the image contained in any given fragment is less detailed, or fuzzier.

The question arises: are human beings simply the tools of the gods? No. The fear that we are being manipulated by divinity is based on the misconception that gods and humans are separate, when in fact they are two parts of a whole. Is the left side of your body the "tool" of the right side? Are your legs merely a way for your arms to travel? These fears of being controlled by divinity arise when we are thinking dualistically, rather that holistically. Humans and deities are interdependent.

Are we human beings on a spiritual path, or divine beings on a human path? The truth is we are both. The transformation of divine consciousness takes place through living consciousness. Consciousness can't change without something to process it; living creatures process consciousness. For a god to be "alive," to be growing and evolving, there must be a living creature tuned into that deity's wavelength. Most people are unaware that they are tapped into at least one, if not several, deity consciousnesses at any given time. Religion is the science of becoming aware of those wavelengths and strengthening our ability to tune them in—through prayer, meditation, etc. Magic is the art of using that awareness for transformation (through ritual and deliberate action). First we transform ourselves, and then our transformed selves effect changes in the physical world.

RELATING TO DEITIES

When you tune in to a deity's consciousness, that deity (who is living simultaneously in all the entities throughout the universe who are also tuned in to it) notices you. Whatever you think may become a part of its memories, just as its thoughts may enter your awareness. You can talk to each other. Gods are the products of the thoughts of all those who share a particular mode of awareness. War gods influence, and are influenced by, the soldiers who embody them. Love goddesses are influenced by the lovers who channel them, and vice versa. Animal spirits represent the collective consciousness of particular types of animals.

There are some deities who have not yet been named by humans. The ones we know through the various mythologies and religions are the ones who have an interest in interacting with the human sphere. Consciousness expresses itself through countless deities, angels, elementals, spirits, devas, ghosts, etc., each of which has its own personality and its own agendas. When you encounter such an entity, never forget that, like people, they have their own motives and desires. Befriending such an entity should be approached with the same caution as befriending any new acquaintance.

We are often in the habit of relating to deities only when we need something—protection, wisdom, a blessing, etc. When petitioning a deity, be polite. You wouldn't be rude to a human that you wanted a favor from, would you? Why would you be rude to a non-human? You don't have to grovel, but don't be demanding either. Realize that you might be turned down; deities are not wish-fulfillment machines. You may have to prove yourself, or do something in return for the deity. Do not make any promises to a deity that you are not prepared to keep. Gratuitous flattery is not appropriate either—it just shows that you do not

The Greek Pantheon

have the proper respect for the entity you are dealing with. Deities can tell when you are licking their boots just to play it safe. Don't think they are stupid enough not to recognize insincerity. Insincerity is the single most dangerous attitude you can possess while communing with divinity. If you can't find it in yourself to approach a particular deity with courtesy and respect, then don't bother.

It is better to establish working relationships with deities before you start asking them for things. Show the deity you wish to work with that you are interested in it. (This is precisely what you are doing when you make an offering to a deity. Remember that actions, as well as material gifts, are appropriate.) Get to know your deity, studying their mythological or religious manifestations, and be open to communication with them. If you do petition a deity directly for something, be sure that you:

- Ask for something you can't do for yourself
- Ask for something that is within their power to give
- Are prepared for the possibility that they will ask for something in return

DEITIES AND ARCHETYPES

Archetypes are living, sentient forms of consciousness that express themselves through deities. Deities are living, sentient forms of consciousness that express themselves through individuals. There is an unbroken link from archetypal consciousness to human consciousness. Mythology is a way of describing the activities of collective consciousness using the symbolism of the individual. Mythology is helpful in understanding the self, because the archetypes are more clearly expressed at a collective (deity) level than at an individual level. We can read mythology, relate to deities, and by seeing which ones are similar to us, we can recognize the expression of archetypes within ourselves.

The goal of the Sexual Mysteries is to balance ourselves both within and without. The first step is understanding what the driving forces in our own personalities are, and in those people that we love. The Goat (or Horned God), the Star (or Celestial Goddess), the Earth Mother and the Sky Father are the four archetypes that influence sexual interactions in human beings. These four archetypes evolved from two older archetypes, the Great Mother and the Moon God. All six of these archetypes manifest repeatedly in ancient mythology. As we come to understand these archetypes, both through their deity-manifestations and through our interaction with them, we will also come to a better understanding of ourselves.

ENDNOTES

1. See *Future Memory* by P. M. H. Atwater and *The Holographic Universe* by Michael Talbot for compelling discussions of precognitive abilities.
2. From *The Holotropic Mind: The Three Levels of Human Consciousness and How They Shape Our Lives*, Stanislav Grof, M.D., with Hal Zina Bennett. Harper San Francisco, 1993.
3. The broadcast model of consciousness, in which your brain tunes in one "wavelength" of reality or another, is not accurate in that it implies a separateness from the consciousness field and a source for this field, but it can be a useful analogy for explaining certain concepts.

THREE

The Sexual Mysteries in History and Myth

Τhe Sexual Mysteries are based on four archetypes of divinity: the Goat, the Star, the Earth Mother, and the Sky Father. These archetypes appear in the mythologies of numerous ancient cultures, including those of Egypt, Phoenicia, Assyria, Babylonia, Sumeria, and Greece. However, in order to understand these archetypes and their associated mysteries, we need to trace them back to their origins in the Paleolithic Era.

THE GREAT MOTHER

In Paleolithic times, before humans had domesticated herd animals, we lived together in small hunter-gatherer tribes. The division of labor between the genders was relatively clear: women foraged for edible plants and cared for children, while men provided the tribe with protection and meat (by hunting). At this time, the role of the male in

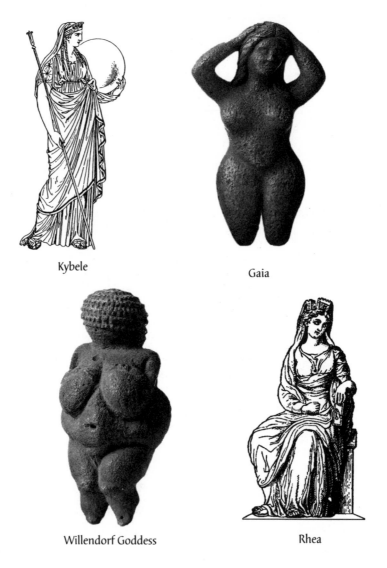

Kybele

Gaia

Willendorf Goddess

Rhea

Aspects of the Great Mother

conception was not understood—humans had not yet made the connection between mating and birth, and it is likely that sexual activity in women occurred at the onset of menstruation, if not before, thus obscuring this connection. As a result, our conception of the Creator was female. Paleolithic humans revered the Great Mother, who was the embodiment of the female power of reproduction. This power was seen as a direct result of woman's ability to menstruate: only women menstruated, and only women conceived. The Great Mother's creative power was not sexual in nature, but rather an inherent quality she possessed by virtue of her femaleness. The mysteries of the Great Mother were the mysteries of birth and death. All creatures, including humans, were seen as children of the Great Mother: humans did not separate themselves from the rest of the animals She had created.

The Great Mother expressed the consciousness that arises from matter: the world and everything in it were created from Her body. She was not exactly a fertility goddess, as has been theorized, but a goddess of abundance. Her gifts were not specifically those of sexual fertility; rather, the Great Mother gave the gifts of fruitfulness. She ensured human survival with a wide variety of healthy plant and animal life, and healthy offspring—all of which were not seen as the result of sexual activity but as a manifestation of woman's creative power.

We can see traces of the Great Mother archetype in the primal mother goddesses Rhea, Gaia, Tiamat, and Kybele.

The worship of the Great Mother was also associated with transvestism, castration, and androgyny or gender confusion. It was thought that the Great Mother's power was an inseparable part of her womanhood. If men wanted to channel this power, they had to make themselves as much like women as possible. This belief was passed down into the Earth Mother tradition, and these practices were retained in the worship of the mother goddesses of later cultures. For example, Kybele's lover Attis castrated himself, and her priests did the same. They also dressed as women and referred to each other in the feminine.

THE MOON GOD

As women explored the mysteries of birth and creation, men were exploring their own mysteries. As hunters, they needed new ways of thinking in order to uniformly describe and measure the world. Men began to measure time in order to determine how much daylight was left before they must return to camp. Like most hunting animals, they began to develop the idea of territory. They began to devise symbolic systems to aid in thinking about and communicating new strategies for catching game. Hunting forced men to pay attention to their supplies, the passage of days, and the distance they had travelled from home. The moon was seen to be of particular importance in the measurement of time, because it changes daily and completes a full cycle in a relatively short period. Thus, early humans used the moon as a tool for tracking the passage of days and months, and for describing the cyclic nature of time. This is why the Moon God, the primal male archetype, is both a hunter and a teacher of systems such as writing, measurement, and the calendar.

We see the vestigial remains of the Moon God archetype in the ancient lunar deities Thoth, Nannar, and Sin.

Sin

Thoth

Aspects of the Moon God

THE BIRTH OF THE SEXUAL MYSTERIES

Animal husbandry was developed at some point in the Paleolithic Era, and with the domestication of herd animals came the realization that men played a crucial role in reproduction. By this time, humans were living both as agriculturalists in stable communities, and as nomadic herding tribes who grazed their animals in the areas surrounding these agricultural settlements.

During this period, the new awareness of male and female sexual roles caused a reevaluation of religious beliefs and gender roles, and four new archetypes of divinity developed. Previously, motherhood was thought to be an inherent female quality; now humans realized that both men and women contributed to reproduction as parents—as woman was mother, so man could be a father—and that both of these roles were a direct result of being initiated into the mysteries of sexuality.

This realization caused consciousness to split again, and sexual activity became a defining factor in social roles. As a result of this split, four archetypes arose—the Goat, the Star, the Earth Mother and the Sky Father (see Figure 3.1). The Goat represented uninitiated male consciousness and the Star represented uninitiated female consciousness, while the Earth Mother and Sky Father embodied female and male consciousness that had been altered via initiation into the Sexual Mysteries. The Star, or Celestial Goddess, and the Goat, or Vegetation God, were the focus of women-only and men-only mysteries, and governed the areas of life that were not geared towards reproduction or child-rearing. Rites involving these two archetypes focused on initiation into the mysteries of each gender. The Star taught young women about menstruation and the arts of agriculture and civilization, and the Goat taught young men about the mysteries of the hunt and the principles of animal husbandry. Both the male and female mysteries would have included preparation for future sexual activity.

The Star and the Goat tended to be expressed in independent individuals, and exemplified the traits that women and men needed to acquire in order to be functional adults within their communities. The

Stage One

Self-awareness is limited. Humans are scavengers and grazers who do not consciously regard themselves as males or females.

Stage Two

Humans are hunters and gatherers. Men specialize in hunting while women focus on gathering. As the lifestyles of men and women diverge, humans become more conscious of the differences between men and women. The archetypes of this time reflect this new division of consciousness.

Stage Three

Humans are herders and cultivators. Awareness of the role of sex in conception is achieved. Two new roles are created. Men are now able to be parents (fathers) and women are now able to become non-parents ("virgins"). This awareness causes the archetypes to split and give rise to four new ones.

Figure 3.1: The Evolution of Human Consciousness

Earth Mother and Sky Father, on the other hand, were specifically focused on the initiation of men and women into parenthood, beginning with conception and continuing through the child-rearing stages. They represented the new phase of life which begins with the commencement of procreative sexual activity and committed sexual relationships. Unlike the Star and the Goat, the Earth Mother and the Sky Father do not live independently—it is their relationship, and the exchange that exists between them (symbolized by their lovemaking) that defines their roles.

The Sexual Mysteries involving these four archetypes are most clearly documented in the religions of ancient Sumeria, Assyria and Babylon. However, we also see mythological traces of these mysteries in the aboriginal religions of pre-Hellenic Greece, Egypt, and Phoenicia. Furthermore, there is evidence that the Sexual Mysteries may have been a part of the early Hebrew tradition. Keep in mind that deities often

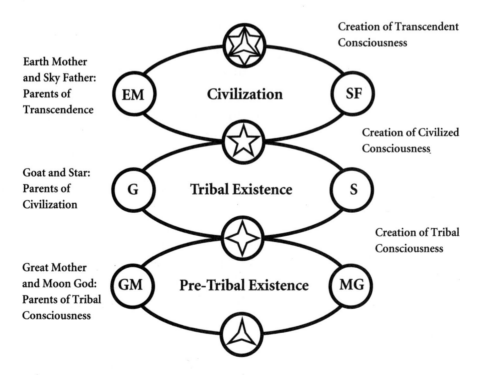

Figure 3.2: The Roles of the Archetypes in the Evolution of Consciousness

have more than one aspect, and that many gods express both the Goat and the Sky Father, and that many goddesses express both the Star and the Earth Mother.

The split in consciousness that produced these four archetypes occurred at a time when agriculture and animal husbandry were beginning to merge, and the cultures associated with these two ways of life were in flux. This merging occurred first in Egypt, then in the Near East, and later still in the Hellenic world. Unfortunately, this split took place in Egypt during such an early period that we have no records of it. Only a few traces of this period survive, buried in the mythologies of later times. However, the Egyptians had close links to the Canaanites, a Ugaritic people in the Near East, and some of the Egyptians' earlier religious beliefs were adopted by the Canaanites. As a result, the Ugaritic texts preserve elements adopted from the Egyptian Sexual Mysteries (elements that were, in Egypt, eventually eclipsed by the expanding cults of Isis and Osiris).

The unique geography of Canaan supported the mix of cultures that gave rise to the Sexual Mysteries, allowing them to flourish for a much longer period of time than they did in other Near Eastern cultures. The land of Canaan was comprised of three climate zones—the first zone was arable land, which supported farming settlements; the second was semi-desert, where nomadic tribes grazed their flocks; and the third was uninhabitable desert. Because of these climate zones, the nomadic herding culture remained stable and the interaction between farmers and herders was extended for a much longer time in Canaan than it was in most other ancient cultures.

In other Near Eastern cultures, the literature of the Sumerians and other peoples offers some information about the development of the four archetypes, but most of this information was written down long after the transition we've described was complete. Greek culture, however, provides us with a great deal of information about this consciousness split, again due to unique geographic and environmental conditions. The Greek province of Arcadia, with its rough climate and rocky soil, was difficult to cultivate and, as a result, the Arcadians were forced to rely on both foraging and animal husbandry as food sources much longer than most other Greeks. For this reason, the merging of agriculture and animal husbandry took much longer in Arcadia. There, the process extended well into classical times and many of the texts documenting this period have survived to the present day.

The Arcadians (who were referred to by other Greeks as "acorn eaters" because of the poor state of their agriculture) were the oldest inhabitants of Greece, and have preserved, along with the primitive living conditions of pre-Hellenic Greece, some of the traditions and beliefs of this area's aboriginal religion.

THE FEMALE ARCHETYPES:
THE STAR AND THE EARTH MOTHER

The Star: Celestial Manifestation of the Divine Feminine

- She is a warrior goddess, often ferocious, and usually acting independently of male authority.
- She is a virgin in the ancient sense: she was not married, and her sexuality is her own. The men around her had no control over her reproductive abilities. She is not necessarily (or even usually) celibate, and is often worshipped through sacred prostitution.
- Although she is sexually active, she seldom has children. In the instances where she is a mother, she fills that role in a biological sense only—she does not raise the children she has given birth to.
- She is associated with either the Moon and/or the stars, and is almost always linked to the planet Venus (as the morning and evening stars).
- She is associated with the formation of laws, both natural and social, and is often seen as a judge. She can be a force of justice and retribution.
- She is associated with animal husbandry, and is often prominent in cultures that depend heavily on domesticated animals for sustenance.

The Earth Mother: Terrestrial Manifestation of the Divine Feminine

- She is a huntress, often called "Lady of the Beasts" and considered to be a protectress of wild animals. Most of her hunting companions were women.

- She is a goddess of procreative sexuality and fertility, and was often worshipped, in ancient times, through the Sacred Marriage ceremony.

- She is a goddess of childbirth and motherhood, and in later times, a goddess of marriage. She is very protective of her children.

- She is associated with the king, and is the source of his authority. Kings were often depicted as sitting on her lap, which served as his throne. The Earth Mother's approval of his reign was publicly demonstrated through the Sacred Marriage ceremony.

- She is a goddess of agriculture, worshipped most prominently in cultures that depend primarily on cultivated crops for sustenance.

When the relationship between sex and reproduction was discovered, the Great Mother of Paleolithic times was split into two archetypes: the Star, whose sexuality was her own, and the Earth Mother, who had been initiated into motherhood.

Many of the ancient goddesses were not limited to being just a Star or just an Earth Mother. Most of these goddesses were originally both, expressing both the celestial and the terrestrial aspects of the female psyche, but at some point in time, many of these goddesses were reduced to one or the other. Some, like Artemis, came to be thought of as exclusively celestial while others, like Hathor, came to be viewed as terrestrial in nature. Eventually, only a few goddesses, such as Ishtar, managed to retain both aspects. Why did this change occur? Why should some goddesses lose their Earth Mother aspect? Why should others lose their Star qualities?

As the fact of paternity became more apparent to ancient peoples, the role of men as fathers grew more important. Before a man's part in conception was understood, humans were matrilineal, tracing lineage through the mother. Lineage determined inheritance, with possessions being passed from mother to daughter; possessions were wealth, conferring status and social power. However, with the development of the mysteries of reproduction, men began to see that this system put social power in the hands of women. If lineage were to be traced through the father rather than the mother, then men would be the ones inheriting and caring for the wealth of their families, rather than women.

There was only one problem with a patrilineal system: maternity is obvious, but paternity is uncertain. How could a man be sure that he really was the father of his partner's children? When men confronted this issue, control of women's reproductive abilities—and therefore, women's sexual behaviors—became extremely important to them.

How did this need to control women's sexuality influence the development of the Star and the Earth Mother? In order to understand this, we must consider each of the two female archetypes carefully. Most goddesses possessed attributes of both the Star and the Earth Mother. The Earth Mother aspect was easiest to control, as she is, in part, defined by her character as a parent. Her fertility is not an inherent trait, but is dependent on male cooperation. Men realized that a woman's power of motherhood could be taken away from her through the withholding of sex. Monogamy was instituted, and women who wished male cooperation in conception had to conform to social rules that ensured the paternity of their children.

The Star was a bit more difficult to control. She was not only sexually independent, but also a ferocious warrior. However, new social rules were now being formed. A new morality arose in which a woman who chose to be a mother was pressured to be faithful to a single mate, and a woman who chose not to be faithful to a single mate was pressured to be chaste. As a result, many of the goddesses who retained their Star nature and resisted attempts to control their sexuality (like Artemis) were remade in the image of the Eternal Virgin. The Star, who was once a sexually independent woman with the right to choose her lovers at will and leave them as she desired, became a woman who traded her sexual freedom for her right to remain independent of male control. As a result, we now have few god-desses who are truly balanced. Most are either predominantly Stars or Earth Mothers, with very little overlap. However, if we look far enough back in the mythological records, we can uncover traces of both the Star and the Earth Mother in most ancient goddesses.

MYTHOLOGICAL MANIFESTATIONS OF THE STAR AND THE EARTH MOTHER

Artemis

The Greek goddess Artemis, like Pan, originated in Arcadia and was later imported to Greece at a very early stage. Later, she was heavily influenced by the imported Semitic goddess Ishtar. Artemis was a virgin goddess, and more than one male in Greek myth was punished for attempting to infringe upon her sexual independence (Actaon being only the best-known example). She roamed the woodlands, leading her band of women on a perpetual hunt.

In addition to being a huntress, there is evidence that Artemis may, in early times, also have been a warrior goddess. At Agrae in Attica, 500 she-goats were sacrificed annually to Artemis Agrotera in thanks for her help at the Battle of Marathon.[1] She was worshipped as a warrior in Laconia: the Spartans sacrificed a she-goat to Artemis Agrotera before any battle or campaign.[2] In Messina, we find a statue of Artemis bearing shield and spear; coins from Laodicea depict an armed Artemis.[3] Her function as a warrior goddess was later transferred to Athena by the invading Hellenic tribes. As a member of the Olympian pantheon and the daughter of Zeus, Athena was answerable to Zeus and the other gods in a way that the pre-Hellenic Artemis was not.

Although Artemis is now seen as being exclusively celestial, this celestial nature was a relatively late addition. Artemis did not assume lunar qualities until her brother, Apollo, began to assume solar qualities. Homer, in fact, does not refer to her at all as a lunar goddess.[4]

As an Earth Mother with ties to the Great Mother archetype, Artemis was both a goddess of the hunt and a protectress of wild animals (the stag was sacred to her). In ancient Greece it was customary, when hunting, to occasionally set free a captured animal in Artemis' honor.[5] Her companions on the hunt were nymphs who had chosen her way of life, and occasionally male hunters, like Orion, who were willing to respect her independence. There are variants of both the Orion and

Artemis as the Huntress, astride a stag

Actaon myths that indicate both of these hunters may originally have been lovers of Artemis,[6] and that their respective deaths were added in later myths by a culture that had a vested interest in maintaining the virginity of independent women.

As animal husbandry became more widely established, Artemis developed ties to herding and crop cultivation. As Artemis Hemerasia she was associated with the domestication of animals, and in some places she was given the epithet "Tauropolos," which means "bull-tender." In her homeland of Arcadia, Artemis was associated with Demeter and Demeter's daughter Despoina; and in Attica she was considered to be a goddess of fruits at the Feast of Thargalia.[7]

Artemis is also a goddess of childbirth, and her association with birth reflects her role as an Earth Mother. One of her sacred animals was the bear, which was a symbol of motherhood in ancient Greece.[8] The myth of Artemis and Kallisto, in which Artemis turns the pregnant Kallisto into a bear before the nymph gives birth, is another remnant from the time when Artemis' terrestrial character was understood. At Brauron, young women participated in initiatory rites under Artemis' direction, and while undergoing these rites the young women were referred to as "bears," indicating that these rites were sexual in nature and involved preparation for motherhood.[9] Another of her epithets translates as "opener of the womb," and early myths show Artemis being connected with loss of virginity. Euripides claims that, in her aspect as Artemis Lochia, this goddess "would not speak to childless women." Her virginal character was a relatively late addition—the original meaning of her epithet "Parthenos" was "unmarried." Sexual rites and dances (probably similar to the style we know as belly dance) were a part of her worship at Ephesus and at Elis.[10]

Artemis' attributes as an Earth Mother are also suggested by her links to other deities. She shares a common place of origin with Pan, the Arcadian Goat, and she obtained her hunting dogs from him.[11] In her aspect as Selene, she had a joint cult in Arcadia with Pan, and may even have been his lover at a very early time. As noted above, Artemis is also worshipped alongside Demeter in Arcadia, and may at some point have

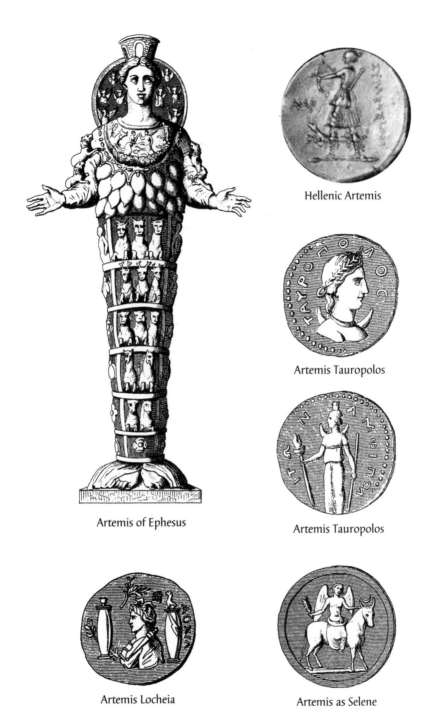

Hellenic Artemis

Artemis of Ephesus

Artemis Tauropolos

Artemis Tauropolos

Artemis Locheia

Artemis as Selene

Some of the varied roles and representations of Artemis

been considered Demeter's daughter (the Greek playwright Aeschylus depicts Artemis as such). The Greeks were not the only people to suggest this relationship. Egyptian myth claims that Artemis is the daughter of Dionysos and Isis (Isis being the Egyptian equivalent of Demeter). At Corone in Messina, Artemis and Dionysos shared a temple, and in Lydia she was worshipped by bands of maenads in laurel groves.[12]

As to the origin of Artemis, there are some indications that she may have been the deity of the Leleges and the Lydians, who were the pre-Hellenic inhabitants of Ephesus. The Leleges had migrated to Ephesus from Crete, where the Earth Mother was worshipped as Ariadne Aphrodite. Pausanias, the Greek historian, claims that when the Hellenic invaders came to Ephesus, they allowed the existing temple to continue to function and adopted the goddess already worshipped there under the name of their own Artemis.[13] Artemis at Ephesus was considered to be a Hellenized form of the Near Eastern Earth Mother, and was thought by the ancient Greeks to be equivalent to the Persian goddess Anaitis, who was also worshipped through sexual rituals.[14]

Ishtar (Astarte/Tanit/Mylitta/Belit)

Ishtar was the "Queen of Heaven," worshipped by the Assyrians and Akkadians. In Carthage, she was known as Tanit, in Babylon she was Mylitta, and the Canaanites called her Belit. Her other epithets include "lioness of heaven" and "the peerless daughter of the moon."[15] The emblem of Ishtar was the eight-pointed star (which was displayed on the gates of the city of Babylon), and she was associated with the planet Venus (as the morning and evening stars).

Ishtar's Star nature was quite evident. She was extremely independent, and often uncontrollable by man and god alike. In spite of the fact that she was married, in Assyrian mythology, to the god Ea, he was unable to curb her wild behavior. As a warrior goddess, she was ferocious. One myth describes how she once went on a rampage, killing man and god alike, devastating the countryside for miles. People prayed to the gods to stop her in her frenzy, but Marduk and the others were afraid to intervene for fear that she would kill them too. Marduk finally came up with a plan: the gods drugged a cup of blood and gave it to her to drink. She fell asleep, and when she awoke, the frenzy was gone.

Ishtar was also associated with the law, and was the keeper of a number of *me* (Sumerian laws of the universe), which she entrusted to Erech, her favorite city. By giving humans possession of the *me*, Ishtar gave them the arts of civilization—the knowledge of weaving, spinning, pottery-making, agriculture, and other arts. She was the "Righteous Judge," "Celestial Ruler," and the "Framer of All Decrees."[16]

Like Artemis, Ishtar was probably not originally a celestial deity, and may not have assumed her lunar attributes until after the seventh century B.C.E. The Moon, in both Babylonian and Assyrian mythology, was considered to be male (in the form of the Moon god Sin, also called Nannar).

As daughter of the Moon, her title "Queen of the Heavens" referred not to her literal position in the pantheon, but to the far-reaching extent of her power. She was not limited to reigning over a specific realm, like the sea or the Moon, but was powerful enough to move freely between heaven and earth. It is possible that when the Assyrians came into contact with the Egyptians, they noticed the similarities between the Egyptian Earth Mother Isis and their own Ishtar, and mistook the solar disk that Isis wears on her forehead for a full moon. These Assyrians may have begun attributing lunar qualities to Ishtar as a result of this misunderstanding of Isis' attributes.[17]

Evidence for Ishtar's terrestrial nature abounds. She was worshipped through sexual rites and sacred prostitution for thousands of years, and the stories that grew up around this goddess had a tremendous influence on the religious practices of many later cultures including Egypt, Crete, Asia Minor, and Greece. She was also a tremendous force in shaping the Judeo-Christian religious tradition, and hence in shaping our current gender roles. Most of the religious ideology regarding women's behavior and women's relationship to the Divine in Judaism and Christianity was formed as a direct reaction to the practices of Ishtar's worshippers. The relevance of this goddess to our current gender predicaments cannot be emphasized enough. Most of Western civilization's ideas about gender roles were formed in the conflict between the Hebrew tribes and Ishtar's worshippers, and passed down to us via Christianity and Islam. To understand Ishtar and why she was dangerous to the Judeo-Christian religious tradition is to understand where our own beliefs about male and female roles come from.

Like Artemis in her Earth Mother aspect, Ishtar was also called "the opener of the womb." Because of her role as patron of Sacred Prostitution, the ancient Hebrews called Ishtar "the Great Whore" and "the Mother of Harlots."

Interestingly enough, there are cylinder seals excavated from the ruins of the Sumerian city Lagash (dated ca. 2300 B.C.E.) which depict Ishtar squatting over the body of her consort in a pose identical to that associated with Kali, the Indian goddess of sexuality, as she squats over the corpse of her lover Shiva.[18] This engraving, along with other evidence, suggests that the worship of Ishtar may have direct links with the Tantric tradition of India, and may, in fact, be a Mesopotamian interpretation of Kali.

Ishtar's link to both agriculture and animal husbandry is clear. She is associated with the Bull of Heaven, which was her father Anu's terrestrial manifestation. When Anu wanted to punish someone, he sent the Bull of Heaven to deal with them. As the Phoenician Astarte, Ishtar assumed the bull's head as a symbol of supreme power.

Inanna

Inanna, the Sumerian mother goddess, is often treated as if she were merely a Sumerian equivalent to Ishtar. However, Ishtar's most prominent attributes are those of the Star, while Inanna, on the other hand, was originally an Earth Mother. It is only later, after centuries of Akkadian and Assyrian domination in Sumeria, that these two goddesses were merged into one deity.

Ishtar was the warlike goddess of the nomadic Akkadian herders, while Inanna was the love goddess of the agriculturalist Sumerians. Ishtar was the goddess of sexual love and "courtesan of the gods,"[19]

Aphrodite

Ariadne

Ishtar

As Star or Earth Mother, the Goddess exhibits beauty and power

worshipped through ritual prostitution, while Inanna was the goddess of marriage, whose worship culminated in the Sacred Marriage between herself (represented by one of her priestesses) and the king of the city. In this capacity, she was, like most Earth Mothers, a legitimizer of the throne. It was only through her approval that any king ruled, and for this reason she was often called "Mistress of Kingship."

Inanna was a goddess of civilization. Her jewelry and clothing were symbols of her power,[20] and her priests were called "linen-wearers."[21] At first, Inanna refused to marry the shepherd Dumuzi because she didn't want to wear his rough woolen clothing. It was only through Dumuzi's own description of the milk and cream produced by his flocks that she was persuaded to wed him. Inanna is the "Queen of Vegetation," and lettuce is sacred to her, as it is to the Egyptian god Min.[22]

Inanna also possessed a celestial side. Her name literally translates as "Queen of Heaven." Like Ishtar, Inanna was called the "Queen of all the *Me*," which she gave in the form of the arts of civilization. Although she was not a Moon goddess at this time (her lunar characteristics were a later addition), she was often compared to this celestial body. She "shines forth like the moonlight," and was often said to be "like heaven."[23]

Ariadne

Ishtar was brought by Phoenician traders to Crete, where she was worshipped as Ariadne. Classical mythology portrays Ariadne as the Cretan princess who helped Theseus kill the Minotaur and free the Athenians from paying human tribute to King Minos of Crete. However, the classical myths were not written by the Cretans who worshipped Ariadne, but by the Greek-speaking peoples who conquered Crete. Very few of the myths of ancient Crete survive, and most of our knowledge of their cultures comes to us filtered through the mythology of the Greeks.

Ariadne was also linked with the bull god Dionysos, whom she was supposed to have married on the island of Naxos after being deserted by Theseus. There is further evidence of Ariadne's link with Dionysos. At least once, she was depicted as the leader of a band of maenads.[24] In one of the villas excavated at Pompeii, the Villa of the Mysteries, we find a series of friezes in which Ariadne and Dionysos jointly oversee what is interpreted to be an initiation rite.[25]

Aphrodite

There is evidence to suggest that the worship of Aphrodite was imported to Attic Greece by Theseus, who learned of her (by the name Ariadne) during his visit to Crete.[26] In some variants of the myth, Theseus did not abandon Ariadne on the island of Naxos, and instead is said to have brought her back to Greece with him. In these variants, Ariadne is said to have introduced a statue of Aphrodite to Delos, and to have figured prominently there as a priestess of Aphrodite, participating in the Delian dances and other festivals of this love goddess. Ariadne was also supposed to wear the crown of Aphrodite, which she retrieved from the bottom of the sea during the trip to Greece. Both Ariadne and Aphrodite were pictured on Attic vases with the epithet "the most holy" (which was also an epithet of the Semitic goddess Qadesh, who was an aspect of Ishtar).[27]

In classical myth, we find traces of this link between Theseus and the importation of Aphrodite into Greece. Before he departed for Crete, Theseus went to the Delphic Oracle for advice, and was told to ask Aphrodite to serve as his guide for the voyage. In thanks for this advice, Theseus sacrificed a she-goat to Aphrodite. Although this myth is probably a later story, created as a means of rationalizing Theseus' ties to Aphrodite, it represents another link between the Cretan and the Greek goddesses.

Aphrodite was another Earth Mother who was worshipped through sexual rites, although much of the meaning in her worship had been lost in the translation from the Near East to Crete, and then from Crete to Greece. In later times, the temples of the Greek love goddess had become mere brothels. Even so, the mythology surrounding Aphrodite still contains many of the original elements found in the Semitic sexual mystery cults. For example, like Ishtar, Aphrodite also had a youthful lover who represented the vegetative spirit (Adonis), and when this youth was killed by a boar, all plant life withered, and Aphrodite mourned him.

The rites surrounding the myth of Aphrodite and Adonis are very similar to the rites surrounding Inanna and Dumuzi.

Aphrodite is best known for her terrestrial aspect, in her role as a goddess of love, but traces of her celestial nature are detectable. Aphrodite sometimes bears the title Ourania, a literal translation of Ishtar's epithet "Meleket Aschamaim," which means "queen of the heavens."[28] Furthermore, Aphrodite Ourania was worshipped by the Spartans and other Greeks as a warrior goddess.

Hathor

The worship of Hathor is so old that we have no records describing the period in which she originates. We only have inferences based on archaeological finds and traces of her original character as they survive in the later iconology and mythology of ancient Egypt. Hathor was the Sky-Cow, or Cow of heaven, and she was often represented either as a cow, or as a woman wearing a crown of cow horns and a sun disk. Like Artemis, Hathor was also a goddess of childbirth.

Hathor was the Egyptian goddess of sexual love, and was worshipped by hierodules (temple prostitutes), much like Ishtar. She was also called the "Lady of Byblos."[29] When the Greeks first came into contact with Hathor, they identified her with their own Aphrodite (and both Hathor and Aphrodite bear the epithet "golden").[30]

Hathor's Star aspect is seldom emphasized. As the daughter of Re, she was associated with the sun, and her titles include "lady of the sky" and "lady of heaven" (the same titles borne by Ishtar and other celestial Semitic goddesses). In her manifestation as Sekhmet, the "eye of Re," Hathor was associated with Ishtar. Like Ishtar, Hathor-Sekhmet also went into a battle fury, laying waste to everything she came across, until she, too, was tricked by one of the other gods into drinking a mixture of beer and pomegranate juice. Whether this story originated with Ishtar or with Hathor-Sekhmet is not known, but it does establish this Egyptian goddess' celestial warrior nature and her ferociously passionate character.

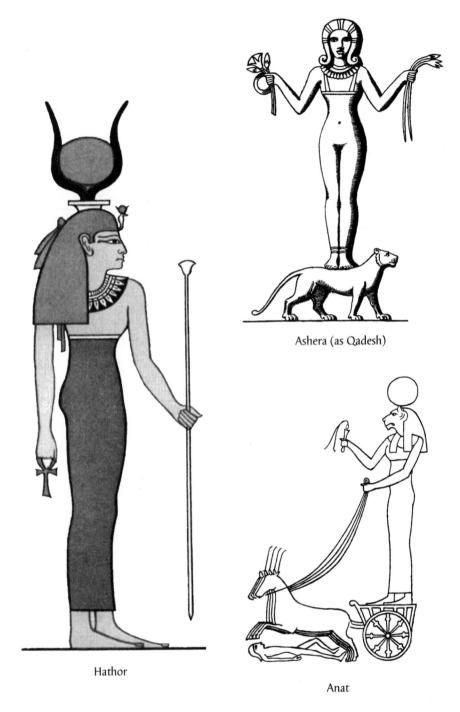

Ashera (as Qadesh)

Hathor

Anat

The archetypal Goddess, fierce as She is nurturing.

39

Anat

Anat was a fierce-tempered warrior goddess, the Star of the Canaanite pantheon. Like the Akkadian Ishtar, she was a huntress and a berserker who gloried in the bloodlust of battle. Like Inanna, she was referred to as the "Queen of Heaven." She was also a sacred prostitute, and her priestesses were the keepers of the Sexual Mysteries in Canaan.

Anat's consort was Baal, the Canaanite equivalent of Adonis, Attis, Dumuzi, and Tammuz. Every year, after his death, Anat would return fertility to the land by journeying to the Netherworld to slay Death (Mot) and return Baal to the land of the living. When Baal replaced El as the King of Gods, he married El's wife Asherah, and Anat's cult began to be absorbed by the cult of Asherah.[31] Eventually, Asherah assimilated most of Anat's properties, and these two deities came to be considered the same goddess.

Asherah

Asherah was the wife of El, King of the Gods of Canaan. She was the mother of all the gods (except for El and Baal), and was worshipped in Canaan from at least 2000 B.C.E. until after 700 B.C.E.[32] Like Hathor and Sekhmet, Asherah was associated with the lion. At some point, her cult came to Egypt, where she was assimilated into the cult of Hathor (who was also an Earth Mother). In her manifestations as Qadesh ("the Holy One," who was eventually assimilated by Ishtar), Asherah was exported to Egypt and paired with the Egyptian god Reshep, with whom she performed the Sacred Marriage rite.[33]

Asherah was also worshipped by the Hebrew tribes after their escape from Egypt (see Yahweh). At the temple in Jerusalem, her worship included male prostitutes who impregnated barren Hebrew wives in her name.[34] Asherah was a goddess of fertility, and was originally separate from Anat, the Canaanite goddess of sexual love. However, due to the political struggles between the followers of El and Baal, these goddesses were eventually merged.

The Male Archetypes:
The Goat and the Sky Father

The Goat: Terrestrial Manifestation of the Divine Masculine

- He is a hunter, even in cultures where herding has replaced hunting as a means of obtaining meat.

- He is a shepherd, even in cultures that were primarily agricultural and had integrated animal husbandry with farming practices.

- He is associated with a horned animal, and in some cases he has horns as well.

- He is a god of fertility, especially animal fertility, symbolizing his link with animal consciousness.

- He is a vegetation god, symbolizing his link with vegetal or plant consciousness.

- He is often represented as ithyphallic (having an exaggerated, erect penis).

- He usually has some sort of connection with an Earth Mother: most frequently he is both her son and her lover. In these cases he may be a sacrificed or dying god, and may be associated with castration, transvestism, and gender confusion.

- He is a youth.

The Sky Father: Celestial Manifestation
of the Divine Masculine

- He is a storm god, associated with thunder, lightning and mountains. Often, the lightning bolt is his symbol of authority, and will be seen as a force of fertility.

- He is a war god.

- He is the King of the Gods.

- He is the Father of the Gods, even when genealogy indicates that he is a second or third-generation deity: he is Father in the social sense, not in the biological sense.

- He is the upholder of both social and universal law, and is often seen as the ultimate judge.
- He is married, and his worship usually involves some form of the Sacred Marriage rite.

As ancient peoples began to understand the implications of the male role in reproduction, the need for a new model of maleness grew. As a result, the Moon God was split into two archetypes: the Goat and the Sky Father. Each of these archetypes contained parts of the old Moon God, but they were also polarized around the act of sexual intercourse. Sex and paternity became the line that separated the Goat from the Sky Father, and was a factor in defining social roles. The Goat's sexuality was that of the unfettered individual, while the Sky Father was one who had been initiated into the role of parent—and into civilization itself—through sexual interaction.

However, just as the Star and the Earth Mother were affected by the social conditions of developing civilizations, so were the Goat and the Sky Father. The Sky Father is the best-known archetype of divinity today. The Christian god, Jehovah, the Hebrew god, Yahweh, and the Islamic god, Allah, are the most prominent Sky Fathers in modern religion. Zeus is one of the most famous Sky Fathers of ancient times, and early Christians drew heavily on the Greek understanding of the Sky Father archetype when describing Jehovah.

Over the centuries, the Sky Father has been tied to the struggle for social power, and comes to us today in a distorted form. When men realized that patriliny was a path to social power, they used the new archetype of the Sky Father as a means of establishing control over women's sexuality. They began to elevate the Sky Father, identifying themselves with this archetype, and to denigrate the Earth Mother. The Earth Mother is the feminine manifestation of terrestrial energy. In their attempts to disassociate themselves from her terrestrial nature, men also began to deny their own terrestrial aspect, the Goat. In this way, the Goat became the shadow side of civilized male consciousness.

In spite of this suppression, the Goat can still be seen in both ancient and modern culture. For example, he appears in the sexual double standard which requires women to be completely faithful to their husbands but allows husbands to have extramarital sex with relatively little consequence. Zeus displays his Goat nature in his innumerable illicit affairs with various women (not to mention the two "wives" he had before he married Hera). The only consequence of Zeus' unfaithfulness is Hera's anger. Hera, on the other hand, although depicted as a scheming shrew and an insufferable nag, is never once said to be unfaithful to Zeus, even by her worst detractors.

Yahweh/Jehovah's suppressed Goat aspect is also apparent—the Judeo-Christian god completely demonizes his Goat aspect as Satan. The Christian Devil still retains his Goat characteristics, from the horns on his head to the cloven hooves which are his feet.

The Sky Father does not need to be an oppressor, though. When balanced by the Earth Mother and her terrestrial nature, he is the driving force behind civilization. He is the teacher, the builder, the leader, the guardian of justice, and the bringer of peace and prosperity. When he is willing to accept his Goat aspect, he embodies everything that is positive about masculinity.

Mythological Manifestations of the Goat and the Sky Father

Pan

Pan is one of the few deities found in ancient mythology who expresses the Goat as his primary aspect. The cult of Pan was native to Arcadia, and was imported to mainstream Greece via Athens in 490 B.C.E., shortly after the Battle of Marathon.[35] Although Pan was both a shepherd and a hunter, hunting was no longer a main source of sustenance in Arcadia, so Pan's hunter aspect was secondary. Herding, however, was a tremendous part of daily life in Arcadia due to the rough climate, and shepherds held a central position in Arcadian society. As a shepherd, Pan represents the link between human and animal consciousness. He is the form the Goat takes in a culture that depends primarily on hunting and herding for sustenance. The story of Pan's introduction to mainstream Greece is also the story of the integration of animal husbandry and agriculture.

Pan had links to a number of other deities in the Greek pantheon. He was linked to the moon through his affair with the nymph Selene (who was eventually linked with Artemis), and they had a joint cult in Arcadia. Pan's relationship with Selene is symbolic of the relationship between the Goat and the Star.

Pan was also associated with Hermes, who was said to be his father. Hermes was Arcadian, but had been assimilated into mainstream Greece much earlier than Pan. Interestingly enough, in his Arcadian homeland, Hermes was also seen as having goat-like characteristics (horns, hooves, fur). When he joined the Olympian pantheon, he lost his goat-like character and assumed a more human appearance. Pan's mother was said by some to be Amaltheia, the Cretan goat goddess who suckled Zeus near Mount Ida. In this mythological tradition, Pan and Zeus are foster brothers.

Pan was also linked to Dionysos, who was a bull god. In hunting and herding cultures the Goat is often depicted as a goat or ram, but in agricultural cultures it is usually symbolized by another horned creature: the bull. Pan appears in Greek art in the company of Dionysos and his Maenads, and it is possible that his Satyrs were a part of the Dionysian revels.[36]

Pan was not only connected with Greek deities, but with those of other cultures as well. As early as the time of Herodotus, the ancient Greeks were equating Pan with the Egyptian Mendes,[37] who was also a horned god. Mendes was called the "All-god." Interestingly enough, Pan means "all" in Greek. The rites of Mendes were sexual, indicating that he, too, was a god of both fertility and virility. We may never know whether or not Pan was really a form of Mendes, imported to Arcadia from Egypt, or whether they are merely parallel manifestations of the same archetype. But either way, the similarities are interesting. Pan was also associated with the rites of Kybele (an Earth Mother), which were

Pan, an almost purely goat-like deity

also sexual in nature. Pan is usually represented as being ithyphallic, reflecting the large part that sexuality plays in their character.

Pan's sexuality is one of his defining characteristics. It is interesting to note that although Pan is depicted as having numerous affairs with various nymphs, he (like the other Greek gods) has few offspring. The few children that do result from his sexual encounters are raised by others—Pan is their father in the biological sense only. Pan's sexuality does not involve initiation into the social aspects of parenthood.

Dionysos

Dionysos was another manifestation of the Goat archetype, incorporated (like Pan) into the Greek pantheon after the Olympians had gained ascendancy. Dionysos was imported from Phrygia, the homeland of Kybele, and is even more closely linked with this Great Mother than Pan. Dionysos was said to have been initiated into the cult of Kybele in Phrygia before he began the wandering journey which eventually brought him to Greece. Like the hunting and herding cultures from which he springs, Dionysos was a nomadic god. His worship in Greece, even when settled, was not centered in any one place. The myths that claim his parents to be Zeus and Semele (or Zeus and Demeter) are attempts to integrate this foreign god into an existing religious system, rather than indications of his true origin.

Dionysos had a very sexual nature. In addition to his link to Kybele, he was also associated with the Greek fertility cult of Demeter and Persephone at Eleusis. It is possible that, at Eleusis, Dionysos was depicted as an aspect of Zeus that had been married to a pre-existing Earth Mother cult through the Sacred Marriage. His very name hints at this link: "Dios" is a form of Zeus, and "Nysa" was the name of the place where Persephone was originally abducted.[38]

Dionysos became the Greek god of the vine, and in this aspect we find an even stronger connection between Dionysos and Zeus. In some places, Zeus was worshipped as *Zeus Didymaeus*, "the god of the Vintage," and those who made libations of wine to Zeus in this aspect wore the ivy crown associated with Dionysos.[39] There is also evidence that Dionysos once had a Sky Father aspect. In some ancient rituals, he is referred to as "the Father and the Son." Additionally, his worship was associated with the Sacred Marriage in Athens, where he was married each year to the Queen of Athens during the annual Dionysian festival.

A note of interest: Frazer reports in *The Golden Bough*[40] that the Eleusinian priests of Dionysos rubbed an ointment containing hemlock on their genitals before the ceremony. Hemlock, Frazer notes, has an anesthetizing effect, and he speculates that the priest would therefore be unable to engage in sexual intercourse after having applied this ointment. However, if the dosage of hemlock were small enough, the anesthetic effect of this ointment would not prevent the hierophant from engaging in sexual intercourse, but would (like many of the lotions sold in marital aid catalogs today) actually prolong intercourse by desensitizing the penis just enough to allow the priest to delay ejaculation and prolong arousal. Delaying ejaculation and prolonging arousal are two of the most crucial techniques in sacred sex, as it is in a state of heightened arousal that connection with divinity is easiest to achieve.[41]

Dionysos embodied both the floral and faunal types of terrestrial consciousness: animal consciousness in his manifestation as a bull god, and plant consciousness in his manifestation as a vine god. In both forms, he represents the sources of sustenance of the agricultural society—the bull, or domesticated animal, which provided milk, meat, material for clothing and tools, a means of plowing the fields, and (in some cases) transportation; and the vine (or other plant life), which offered food for humans and animals. Because he embodies terrestrial consciousness manifesting in an agricultural society, he has lost his horns. The guiding force in an agricultural society is the drive towards civilization, in which humans increasingly distinguish between animals and themselves. However, earlier depictions of Dionysos manifest his Goat aspect strongly. His Cretan form, *Dionysos-Zagreus,* was a wild goat with enormous horns.[42]

Although he was intimately connected with fertility, Dionysos' special gift to humankind was viticulture (the making and mixing of wine). Wine in ancient Greece was not just fermented grape juice, but also contained a number of herbs and other substances (some of which may have had mind-altering properties), and was diluted with water to a level safe for consumption.[43] Wine brought inspiration, and was revered by early Greeks as a means of communing with the Divine.

Zeus

Mountain-dwelling Zeus, like most Sky Fathers, was a storm god. Lightning was the symbol of his power, and under the names *Zeus Astrapaios, Zeus Bronton,* and *Zeus Keraunios* he was worshipped as "the Thunderer." In this aspect he was also a warrior (although eventually the Greek goddess Athena and the god Ares took over this function) and was depicted as the Victor and Maintainer of Peace. In this manifestation, he is always shown in the company of Nike, the goddess of Victory.[44]

Zeus is considered to be both the Father of the Gods and the Father of Men, although he is neither in a biological sense.[45] Epictetus says that "all Fathers are sacred to Zeus," and it is in the social sense, as ruler of both men and gods and dispenser of justice, that Zeus fills the role of Father.

He is also a god of marriage (*Zeus Teleios*), and even though the marriage of Zeus and Hera was not depicted as happy, it was frequently reenacted by ancient Greeks in the *hieros gamos*, or Sacred Marriage. Marriage is important to Zeus not for its potential to make its participants happy, but for its usefulness as a tool for social control by enforcing monogamy, and thereby ensuring paternity. Zeus' concern with paternity was expressed in his epithets of "Genethlios" (the god of the birthright) and "Herkios" (the protector of families). As paternity determines descent, and therefore inheritance, Zeus is also a god of family property. He was called *Zeus Ktesios* (the protector of family property) and *Zeus Klarios* (the god of allotments).[46]

In his more positive aspects, Zeus, as King of the Gods, is a leader and a bringer of order. He maintains social peace as *Zeus Homolois* ("the god who holds people in accord") and *Zeus Philios* ("the god of friendship"). He dispenses justice[47] as *Zeus Moiragetes* (the leader of

Tammuz

Adonis

Dionysos

Zeus

As Goat or Sky Father, the God manifests the Divine Masculine.

fate) and *Zeus Enaisimos* (the controller of destiny). He inspired the Athenians to form their city council, and presided over assemblies and trials in the role of judge.

Zeus is said to despise Ares, who, in classical writings, reflects the Goat at his worst—violent, arrogant and irrational. Even so, Zeus demonstrates his own suppressed Goat nature. In addition to his links with Dionysos, Zeus has an insatiable sexual appetite, as demonstrated by his numerous extramarital affairs. In many of these encounters, he seduced the object of his desires by manifesting as a horned animal such as a ram, a goat, or a bull.

Zeus' own origin indicates that his Goat aspect may once have been widely recognized. He was raised by the Cretan goat goddess Amaltheia, and when she died, he used her skin to create the *aegis,* which is his symbol of power.[48] One of his strangest epithets was "Aigophagos," which literally means "the devourer of goats", and probably points to his origin in a culture that depended primarily on herding for sustenance. Zeus' terrestrial nature is also apparent in his manifestation as *Zeus Georgos,* who is a harvest god, and as *Zeus Karpodotes,* who is a vegetation god.

Tammuz (Dumuzi)

In the Near-Eastern mythologies, we see a much clearer picture of the Goat's vegetal form. The best known Near Eastern Goat is Tammuz, lover of the Assyro-Babylonian Ishtar. He is a shepherd,[49] and also a sacrificed god, like Adonis. He arose from the merging of the highly agricultural Sumerian culture and the nomadic Akkadians herders. The Akkadians, after conquering the Sumerians, adopted many of the Sumerian ways in their attempt to govern their new land. As herders, they had no knowledge of agriculture and had to learn it from the Sumerians. Because of this, Tammuz eventually lost his horns, and he is much more closely connected to plant consciousness than to animal consciousness. However, traces of his link to the herding culture remain, and Tammuz sometimes manifests as the astral heavenly bull, referred to as "the pre-eminent steer of heaven."[50]

In his Sumerian form as Dumuzi, this deity was seen as the life force of the grain, and he was killed by Inanna (his spouse in Sumerian mythology). The Sumerian myths may reflect a time when the dying vegetation god (as represented by the king of the land) may have been ritually sacrificed after marriage to the goddess (represented by her priestess). It was his sacrifice that made the fertility of the fields possible, and his willingness to take Inanna's place in the Netherworld during the dry season which allowed humans to survive.

While we have less information about the lessons that Tammuz and Dumuzi offered their worshippers, enough of the details of their worship survive to show us that both of these gods did manifest the Goat archetype, and that the Sexual Mysteries were practiced in the Near East.

Dumuzi (and Tammuz) were primarily reflections of the Goat archetype, but also possessed the beginnings of Sky Father consciousness. Dumuzi was both king of Sumeria, as well a priest in the service of Ishtar, and would have ruled through the divine favor of the goddess.

Adonis

Adonis was another Greek figure who manifested the Goat, albeit in a much more civilized, human form. He was a youth, beloved of Aphrodite. He was also a shepherd, represented the spirit of the grain and other vegetation, and he was a dying god, mourned by his goddess-lover. However, the cult of Aphrodite and Adonis (a derivative of the worship of Ishtar and Tammuz) was imported relatively late in Greek history, and much of the meaning behind his worship may have already been lost by this time. The surface details were retained, but the core practice of sexual initiation had been reduced to a form of sympathetic magic designed to ensure crop fertility.

El

El, the King of the Gods of Canaan, is one of the most positive manifestations of the Sky Father that has survived to modern times. Called "the Father of Men," El was known as "the Kind, the Compassionate."[51]

In his role as "the Father of Time" he was considered to be the ruler of fate. As the supreme sovereign, he was responsible for dispensing justice to gods and humans alike. His celestial manifestation was the sun itself. The rays of the sun were believed to be the hands of El, reaching down to the earth.[52]

Like most Sky Fathers, El was associated with mountains (his epithet "El Shadday" means "God of the Mountain"). However, as a god of civilization, he also sometimes dwelt in a pavilion near the rivers that brought fertility to Canaan. El ensured the fertility of his land through the Sacred Marriage rite in which he ritually copulated with his wife Asherah (who was also "the Lady of the Sea").[53]

El once had a Goat aspect. He was, at one time, a vegetation god, and his most important title was "the Bull."[54] However, as he ascended to become King of the Gods, many of his terrestrial characteristics were suppressed in favor of his Sky Father attributes.

Baal

The Canaanite god Baal, who is frequently mentioned in the Old Testament, was originally a manifestation of the Goat. He was a vegetation god who brought rains to the farmlands of Canaan. Like Dumuzi, his sacred animal was the bull.[55] Baal was second in command to El (the King of the Gods). He was not native to the Canaanite pantheon, but was probably imported by Phoenician traders.

As the lover of Anat (the Canaanite Star), Baal's mythos is related to the Ishtar/Tammuz cycle, in which the sacrificed god was taken to the Netherworld. He was then retrieved by Anat, who journeyed to the Netherworld to slay Baal's adversary Mot. She then brought Baal back to life, thus returning fertility to the land above. Interestingly enough, before he was slain by Mot (who represented the heat of the dry season), Baal mated with a heifer, symbolizing the alternate dependence on agriculture for sustenance during the rainy season and on herd animals during the dry season.[56] It is possible that the Baal cycle preserves, in some form, traces of the Egyptian Sexual Mysteries. His lover, Anat, was worshipped through sacred prostitution, like Ishtar and Hathor.

As Baal became more prominent in the Canaanite pantheon, he began to take over some of El's functions, and assumed a Sky Father aspect. He became a storm god (called "Rider on the Clouds") whose symbol was the lightning.[57] Later, this aspect had become such an important part of his nature that the early Romans referred to him as *Caelus*, which means "sky."[58] He was also a warrior, bearing the epithets "the Conqueror" (similar to Zeus' title "the Victor") and "the Valiant One."

Baal was worshipped in a temple (referred to as his "house"), and we are lucky enough to have found a Ugaritic text that describes his petition for the right to build that house alongside the dwellings of El and the other Canaanite gods. By building himself a house, Baal marked the completion of his transition from Goat to Sky Father (the temple was the mark of the civilized god in early Semitic religions). By the time the Hebrews had returned from their exile in the desert, Baal was winning his struggle to replace El as the King of the Gods, and was on his way to becoming a Sky Father.

As a Sky Father, Baal needed an Earth Mother to serve as his wife. When he took El's position as King of the Gods, Baal also became the husband of Asherah, the Mother of the Gods, leading to confusion between Asherah (his new wife) and Anat (his original wife).

Yahweh (Jehovah)

Yahweh is one of the most famous Sky Fathers, and is worshipped to this day in the Judaic and Christian religions.[59] Like Zeus and Baal, he had a celestial nature, and was a storm god, associated with lightning and thunder. He was a warrior, leading the Israelites in battle against their Canaanite neighbors.

Yahweh was also seen as a civilizing force, giving Moses the Ten Commandments on Mount Sinai, and enforcing numerous cultural taboos among the Hebrew tribes through the Levite priesthood. Like Baal, Yahweh also had a temple made of cedar, reflecting the urbanization of the Hebrews after they settled in Canaan.[60]

Like all other Sky Fathers, Yahweh was married. His mate was Asherah, the Canaanite Earth Mother—the same Asherah who was worshipped by the Canaanites as the husband of El. They were worshipped together as a divine couple for years, as is seen in various Old Testament scriptures.[61] Why would the Hebrew god Yahweh be married to an Earth Mother goddess from another religion? Yahweh was originally El, the Sky Father of the Canaanite pantheon, who was transformed by the reform of Moses into a new deity during the Hebrews' desert wanderings. Yahweh himself confirms this, in *Exodus* 6:2-3:

> *God {Elohim} spoke to Moses and he said to him: "I am Yahweh. I appeared to Abraham, Isaac, and Jacob as El Shadday, but by my name Yahweh I was not known to them.*

"El Shadday," which, as we have seen above, means "God of the Mountain" and is a common epithet of the Canaanite god El. Originally, the Hebrews worshipped El and Asherah as the divine couple. When Moses and the Levite priesthood remade El as Yahweh, they

Yahweh, the predominant Judeo-Christian Sky Father

retained Asherah, remaking her as the bride of the new god. Asherah was worshipped in the Temple at Jerusalem alongside Yahweh until the reforms of the Hebrew king Josiah, at which point the *hakkelim* (cult objects used in the worship of Asherah) were removed from the Temple.[62]

Like many Sky Fathers, Yahweh eventually came to dislike his terrestrial nature and attempted to deny it by divorcing his wife Asherah. However, even when Asherah worship had been eliminated among the Hebrews, Yahweh still had to contend with his own terrestrial aspect. He responded by projecting it onto one of his own angels, creating the Devil. (Before the reforms of Josiah and the removal of Asherah from the Hebrew pantheon, Satan was still seen as an executive officer of Yahweh.) The Devil, who is often ithyphallic like Pan and Min, embodies all that the unbalanced Sky Father fears in his terrestrial nature: sexuality that cannot be controlled, and that has the potential to overwhelm reason, transforming man into beast. The ancient Hebrews understood the power of sexuality to transform consciousness, but did not understand that it is a tool that can either be used correctly or abused.

Min and Amun

As we look even further back, we find that little evidence remains regarding the earliest Egyptian deities. Most of what is known comes from a period after Egypt had made the transition to agriculture as its main means of subsistence. Min (Menu is the Egyptian form of his name) is thought to be the oldest of the Egyptian deities. His worship was established at least as early as 3000 B.C.E.[63] As near as we can tell, he himself was not depicted with horns, but he is associated with a horned animal: the white bull was sacred to him.

His sexual nature, however, is readily apparent. Even in the oldest statues and inscriptions, Min is depicted as ithyphallic, and is usually shown grasping his immense phallus in one hand and a flagellum in another. Even in later times, his sexuality must have been a key component of his personality: records show priests offering long-leaf lettuce to Min, which was supposed to allow him to have sex untiringly.[64] Another clue to his nature is the fact that the ancient Greeks, when coming in contact with Min, equated him with Pan.

Min was eventually assimilated by the god Amun, who was a later ithyphallic Egyptian deity. In this aspect, Amun bore the title "Kamute," which means "Bull of his Mother,"[65] and which may indicate a sexual relationship with an Earth Mother such as Hathor. Amun was associated with both the bull and the ram, and another of his titles was "The Lord of the Two Horns." A third animal sacred to him was the snake, a symbol of reincarnation. As a snake deity, Amun was called by a name that translates as "He Who Has Completed His Moment." In this form, Amun may have been a sacrificed god.[66]

Amun also had a sexual aspect: on certain occasions at Thebes, the Queen was sent to the temple of Amun to become his consort. Her marriage to and subsequent sexual relationship with the god ensured the divinity of her offspring and reinforced their right to rule. This sacred marriage between Amun and the Queen is depicted on the walls

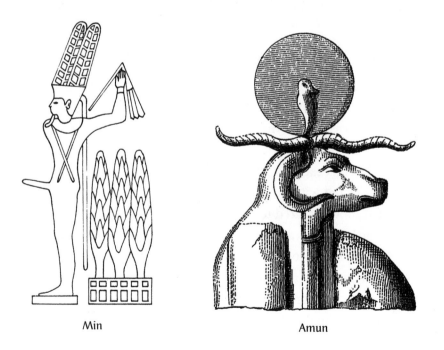

Min

Amun

Min and Amun demonstate the evolving nature of the God.

of the temples at Deir al Bahari and Luxor, which are thought to be two of the oldest surviving temples in Egypt. There is also evidence which hints that priestesses connected to the temple of Amun may have engaged in ritual prostitution. The "concubines of Amun" were not subject to the standard restrictions that Egyptian morals placed on female sexuality, but were said to have led the loosest of lives until puberty, at which point they were married.

Amun also had a celestial nature, most obvious in his designation as a sky god and his association with the Egyptian Sun god Re.[67] He was considered to be the supreme god of the Egyptian pantheon (before Osiris came to power), and in that capacity served as King of the Gods.

THE FOUR ARCHETYPES

As we have seen, the four archetypes have manifested repeatedly throughout history in the religious beliefs of numerous cultures. Each culture expressed these archetypes in the form of deities that were appropriate to their ways of life, but the underlying archetype remained the same. Of course, some deities expressed these archetypes more clearly than others, and most deities manifested more than one archetype at any given time. As one deity was merged with or assimilated by another, the characteristics of these archetypes were spread throughout the mythologies of ancient cultures. In spite of the cultural distortion through which each society expresses these archetypes, these deity forms have survived to modern times, where they are still expressed through our culture. Who does not recognize the figure of the Sky Father in our powerful but sometimes misguided political leaders? The Goat in our highly skilled but often immature sports celebrities? The Earth Mother still cares for her family, while the modern Star wears a three-piece suit instead of armor, and carries a brief-case instead of a sword.

Many of the problems with gender roles in our society stem from our caricatured depiction of these archetypes, and our expression of them via sexual stereotypes. If we are willing to take the time to understand the ancient origins of these stereotypes, we can separate the underlying archetypes from their veneer of cultural prejudice. Once we have done this, we will be free to construct new gender roles for ourselves—roles that express these archetypes in a way that is empowering for both men and women.

ENDNOTES

1. *The Cults of the Greek States: Volume 2*, Lewis Richard Farnell. Aegaean Press, Inc., 1971.

2. Ibid.

3. *Religious Cults Associated with the Amazons*, Florence Mary Bennet. Caratzas Publishing Company, 1987

4. *The Cults of the Greek States: Volume 2*, Lewis Richard Farnell. Aegaean Press, Inc., 1971.

5. Ibid.

6. *Orion: The Myth of the Hunter and the Huntress*, Joseph Fonteniose. University of California Press.

7. *The Cults of the Greek States: Volume 2*, Lewis Richard Farnell. Aegaean Press, Inc., 1971.

8. *The Cult of Pan in Ancient Greece*, Philippe Borgeaud, trans. Kathleen Atlas and James Redfield. University of Chicago Press, 1988.

9. Ibid.

10. *The Cults of the Greek States: Volume 2*, Lewis Richard Farnell. Aegaean Press, Inc., 1971.

11. *Ancient Pagan Symbols*, Elisabeth Goldsmith. G.P. Putnam's Sons, 1929.

12. *The Cults of the Greek States: Volume 2*, Lewis Richard Farnell. Aegaean Press, Inc., 1971.

13. *Religious Cults Associated with the Amazons*, Florence Mary Bennet. Caratzas Publishing Company, 1987.

14. *The Cults of the Greek States: Volume 2*, Lewis Richard Farnell. Aegaean Press, Inc., 1971.

15. *Myths of Babylonia and Assyria*, Donald A. Mackenzie. Gresham Publishing Company.

16. *The Woman's Encyclopedia of Myths and Secrets*, Barbara Walker. Harper and Row, 1983.

17. *The Cults of the Greek States: Volume 2*, Lewis Richard Farnell. Aegaean Press, Inc., 1971.

18. *The Woman's Encyclopedia of Myths and Secrets,* Barbara Walker. Harper and Row, 1983.

19. *New Larousse Encyclopedia of Mythology,* trans. Richard Aldington and Delano Ames. The Hamlyn Publishing Group, 1959.

20. *Greek Myths and Mesopotamia: Parallels and Influences in the Homeric Hymns and Hesiod,* Charles Penglase. Routledge, 1994.

21. *The Sacred Marriage Rite: Aspects of Faith, Myth and Ritual in Ancient Sumer,* Samuel Noah Kramer. Indiana University Press.

22. Ibid.

23. Ibid.

24. Maenads were women who worshipped Dionysos.

25. *The Sacred Prostitute: Eternal Aspect of the Feminine,* Nancy Qualls-Corbett. Inner City Books, 1988.

26. *The Cults of the Greek States: Volume 2,* Lewis Richard Farnell. Aegaean Press, Inc., 1971.

27. *The Sacred Prostitute: Eternal Aspect of the Feminine,* Nancy Qualls-Corbett. Inner City Books, 1988.

28. *The Cults of the Greek States: Volume 2,* Lewis Richard Farnell. Aegaean Press, Inc., 1971.

29. Byblos was also a cult center of the Phoenician Astarte (who was another manifestation of Ishtar).

30. *A Dictionary of Egyptian Gods and Goddesses,* George Hart. Routledge and Kegan Paul, 1986.

31. *Asherah: Goddess of Israel,* Richard J. Petty. Peter Lang Publishing, Inc., 1990.

32. Ibid.

33. Ibid.

34. Ibid.

35. *The Cult of Pan in Ancient Greece,* Philippe Borgeaud, trans. Kathleen Atlas and James Redfield. University of Chicago Press, 1988.

36. In at least one myth, Pan claims to have had sex with all of Dionysos' Maenads, indicating not only a possible link between the two gods, but also hinting that the cult of Pan probably involved some form of sacred sexuality.

37. Mendes was mistakenly described by Herodotus as a being a goat, and this misconception survives into the present day. In actuality, Mendes was represented by the ram.

38. *The Road to Eleusis: Unveiling the Secret of the Mysteries,* R. Gordon Wasson, Carl A.P. Ruck, Albert Hofmann. Harcourt Brace Jovanovich, 1978.

39. *The Cults of the Greek States: Volume 1,* Lewis Richard Farnell. Aegaean Press, Inc., 1971.

40. *The Golden Bough: The Magic Art and the Evolution of Kings*, Sir James George Frazer, vol II. The MacMillan Company, New York, 1935.

41. Alain Danielou, in his book *Gods of Love and Ecstasy*, presents a tremendous body of evidence indicating that Dionysos was a manifestation of the Indian deity Shiva, around whom the cult of Tantra is centered.

42. *The Greek Myths: Volume 1*, Robert Graves. Penguin Books, 1955.

43. *The Road to Eleusis: Unveiling the Secret of the Mysteries*, R. Gordon Wasson, Carl A.P. Ruck, Albert Hofmann. Harcourt Brace Jovanovich, 1978.

44. *The Cults of the Greek States: Volume 1*, Lewis Richard Farnell. Aegaean Press, Inc., 1971.

45. Ouranos, being the first male deity, is literally the Father of the gods, and Prometheus was, according to mainstream Greek mythology, the creator of mankind: Zeus assigned the task to Prometheus after he himself had tried and failed four times to create a suitable race of humans.

46. *The Cults of the Greek States: Volume 1*, Lewis Richard Farnell. Aegaean Press, Inc., 1971.

47. Zeus was also thought to be the father of Dike, the goddess of Justice.

48. *New Larousse Encyclopedia of Mythology,* trans. Richard Aldington and Delano Ames. The Hamlyn Publishing Group, 1959.

49. Dumuzi was a shepherd in death as well as in life: as a chthonic deity, he tended the flocks of the stars, which were thought by the Sumerians to be souls of the dead.

50. *Myths of Babylonia and Assyria,* Donald A. Mackenzie. Gresham Publishing Company.

51. *Stories from Ancient Canaan,* ed. and trans. Michael David Coogan. Westminster Press, 1978.

52. *New Larousse Encyclopedia of Mythology,* trans. Richard Aldington and Delano Ames. The Hamlyn Publishing Group, 1959.

53. Ibid.

54. Ibid.

55. *Stories from Ancient Canaan,* ed. and trans. Michael David Coogan. Westminster Press, 1978.

56. Ibid.

57. Ibid.

58. *Dictionary of Gods and Goddesses, Devils and Demons,* Manfred Lurker, trans. G.L. Campbell. Routledge, 1987.

59. Jehovah is the Christianized form of Yahweh.

60. *Stories from Ancient Canaan,* ed. and trans. Michael David Coogan. Westminster Press, 1978.

61. *Asherah: Goddess of Israel,* Richard J. Petty. Peter Lang Publishing, Inc., 1990.

62. Ibid.

63. *A Dictionary of Egyptian Gods and Goddesses,* George Hart. Routledge and Kegan Paul, 1986.

64. Ibid.

65. Ibid.

66. Ibid.

67. Re, like the Canaanite Sky Father El, is also depicted as a solar disk, with emanating rays which terminate in hands.

FOUR

Polarity and Consciousness

Consciousness has two polarities—the Celestial and the Terrestrial. Celestial consciousness is consciousness focused on the world of thoughts and ideas. Terrestrial consciousness is focused on the physical world and on physical laws and demands.

Everyone has the ability to access these two types of consciousness. The nature of a person's consciousness can be described by examining the degree to which that person focuses on their celestial or terrestrial side.

When someone focuses primarily on celestial consciousness, he or she tends to be very mental and abstract, with his or her "head in the

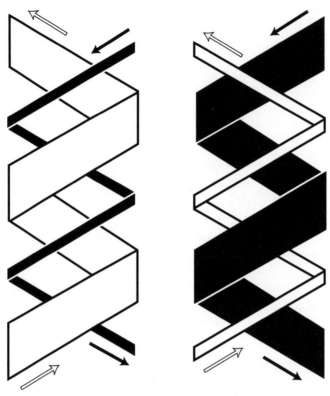

Figure 4.1

clouds." Such a person often becomes frustrated with the practical details and demands of everyday life. When a person focuses primarily on terrestrial consciousness, he or she tends to be very "grounded" and "down to earth." Such a person has difficulty generating new ideas and becoming inspired. These states of consciousness can be understood as the result of two energetic flows within a person—the earth-tide, or descending, terrestrializing flow, and the star-tide, or ascending, celestializing flow.

The earth-tide flows from the top of the head to the toes. The star-tide flows in the opposite direction, from toes to head. Everybody experiences both the earth-tide and the star-tide, but in men the strongest flow tends to be the earth-tide, and in women the strongest flow tends to be the star-tide (Figure 4.1). In other words, men and women tend to be energetically imbalanced.[1]

Shadows

Does this mean that all men are practical and down-to-earth, and all women have their heads in the clouds? No. There is a very big difference between how one's energy is balanced, and how one chooses to use their energies.

In creating a civilization, it is important to have Sky Fathers and Earth Mothers, because the Goat and the Star are very independent, and are not interested in working with others, raising children, or worrying about being socially acceptable. Because of this, civilized humans have strongly divorced themselves from these independent archetypes. We have rejected the Goat, transforming him into "the Devil." The Star, once a proud warrioress, has been disempowered by pressure to remain chaste and meek.

Due to cultural propaganda and societal pressures, most of us choose to focus our consciousness on the energetic mode that is actually most foreign to ourselves. Men are rewarded for being controlled Sky Fathers, while women are pressured and coerced into being docile Earth Mothers. In other words, men and women are cut off from their source of independence and power by social conditioning so that they can be more easily fit into the mold of society. This is not entirely bad: a successful civilization requires people to give up some of their independence. However, it is very important to find a balance between conformity to social rules and expression of personal freedom. We have not achieved this balance yet.

C. G. Jung used the term "shadow" to describe a portion of one's consciousness that has been repressed. For most modern, civilized human beings, the Goat and the Star are our shadow-selves. Some people, however, have the parental archetypes as their shadows, and resist "growing up." In either case, as you begin moving your consciousness to include your shadow, keep in mind that it may be furious with you for having suppressed it. You may have to make amends.

Dealing with Imbalance

Eastern Tantra recognizes that people are energetically imbalanced. However, because it developed in a male-dominated culture, this system is exclusively focused on correcting the imbalance in men. It does this through exercises that increase the star-tide (ascending energy). This ascending energy is termed *kundalini* in the Eastern traditions.

In Eastern Yoga and other traditions that seek enlightenment without sex, the process of raising kundalini is the act of balancing an already-strong earth-tide by increasing the weaker (in most males) star-tide. For thousands of years, men seeking enlightenment have unwittingly struggled to force their star-tide to be stronger (and their earth-tide to be weaker) so that they could achieve a balanced divine or enlightened state of consciousness (see Figure 4.2). Women, attempting the same exercises, may find them ridiculously easy compared to their male counterparts, and have often been made to believe that they weren't doing the exercises correctly because they weren't experiencing enough difficulty (in other words, they weren't experiencing the same sensations encountered by men practicing those exercises).

Most women need to do the opposite—to balance their predominant star-tide by increasing the flow of energy through their bodies in the opposite direction. As you might expect, such "grounding" exercises are often easier for men. These tendencies have been reinforced by thousands of years of social conditioning.

The goal of the following exercises is not to limit you to one tendency or the other, but to enable you to experience both the star-tide and the earth-tide, and to use these energy configurations for personal transformation. In the Sexual Mysteries, each partner strives to make his or her natural energy as strong and vital as possible. Partners then bring these energy flows together in the sex act, where they complement each other and create divine consciousness within both.

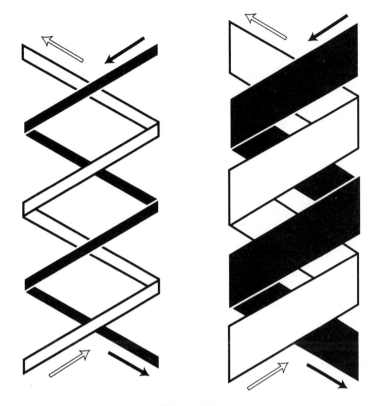

Figure 4.2

TIDAL EXERCISES

The following exercises will teach you to feel and direct the flow of energy through your body in both directions. Even if you don't feel anything at first when you do these exercises (or any of the other exercises described in this book), don't assume that nothing is happening. They are designed to focus awareness on processes that are already occurring in your body so you can deliberately influence these processes. If any exercise makes you feel uncomfortable, try to do it just a little bit longer before stopping. The uncomfortable feeling may fade, to be replaced by a much nicer sensation. If the discomfort persists, then stop.

Because all people have both an ascending and a descending energetic flow, anyone can work at increasing either of these. However, men should not become frustrated if they have difficulty raising energy alone, nor should women become upset if they have difficulty grounding their energy alone. The important thing is to have fun by getting to know your body and learning how energy flows through it.

STRENGTHENING THE STAR-TIDE

A few of the benefits of strengthening the star-tide include increased creativity, increased sensitivity to energy, the awakening of intuitive and psychic powers, and greater ability to think abstractly.

Sit in a comfortable position, keeping your spine straight. Cross your legs if possible. As you breathe slowly and deeply, visualize energy entering your body through your genitals and traveling up your spine. Pay attention to the sensations your body experiences as the energy rises. As it reaches the top of your head, it flows out of your body and rises into the sky.

Maintain this energy flow for a few minutes. Relax. Daydream or pay attention to any spontaneous impressions you receive.

STRENGTHENING THE EARTH-TIDE

Strengthening the earth-tide will increase your physical sensitivity, strengthen your connection to the material, enhance your ability to manifest creativity in the physical plane, help to focus your drive on specific goals, and make it easier for you to think in concrete terms.

Sit in a comfortable position, keeping your spine straight. Place your feet flat against the floor. Breathe deeply (but at a normal pace) and focus on the sensation of energy entering your body through the top or back of your head and traveling down your spine. When the energy reaches your genitals, it flows out of your body and down into the earth.

Maintain this energy flow for a few minutes. Relax. If possible, follow this exercise with some physical activity, such as going for a walk.

BALANCING THE TIDES

Stand or sit in a comfortable position, feet flat against the floor. As you breathe slowly and deeply, visualize energy entering your body from both the top of your head and your genitals, flowing simultaneously up and down your spine. This can be a tricky visualization, and may take some time to learn. If you are having difficulty, try this modification: when you inhale, bring the energy upwards towards the sky; when you exhale, bring the energy back downwards into the earth.

Maintain this energy flow for a few minutes before stopping.

ENERGY CENTERS

The energetic tides are responsible for the formation of the energy centers in the body. In Hindu mysticism, these energy centers are called *chakras*, and are described as spinning wheels in the energetic body. Figure 4.3 is a model for how an ascending and descending flow can create a spinning, wheel-like flow. Energy centers are important for relating to consciousness through the body, and are places in the energy field where ascending and descending energies meet and are integrated.

Your body contains a great number of energy centers. At any point where the earth-tide and star-tide interact, you will find a center, and the two tides interact throughout the entire body. Eastern Yoga has identified seven important sites of interaction, aligned roughly along the spine. These centers are major control points for the physical body. However, you can, through observation and trial and error, identify and work with other points throughout your body. Don't hesitate to experiment.

An important thing to keep in mind is that the energy centers which are higher in the body are more celestial in nature, while the energy centers that are lower in the body are more terrestrial. Focusing awareness on a higher center encourages you to shift your consciousness to a more celestial mode, while focusing on a lower center has the

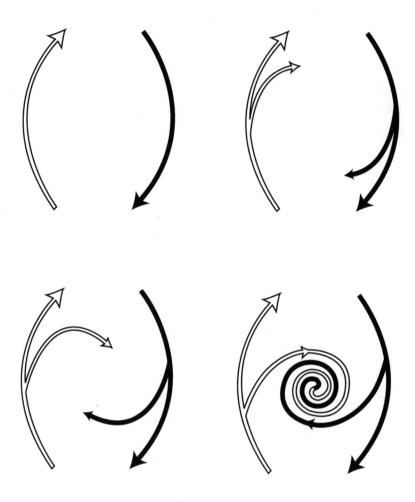

Figure 4.3

opposite effect. If your celestial and terrestrial flows are not balanced, your energy centers will reflect this imbalance.

There are a number of helpful books on working with energy centers.[2] Rather than try to give a comprehensive description of the various beliefs about the energy centers, we've included a brief overview of the seven major ones as they are viewed by the Western metaphysical tradition.

ROOT CENTER: SECURITY AND STABILITY

When your root center is balanced, you are good at finding ways to get your basic needs met while maintaining good relationships with the people around you. If your root center is dominated by the star-tide, you may find yourself openly demanding that the people around you be constantly giving to you. If your root center is dominated by the earth-tide, you may attempt to manipulate the people around you in order to get what you want.

When you make a connection between your root center and your partner's root center, you will find an increase in your sense of security about the relationship, as well as an intensification of the passion between you.

The Western color associated with the root center is red. Herbs that activate this energy center are ashwagandha, haritaki, lotus root, and shatavari.[3] The state of your root center dtermines your ability to express Great Mother consciousness.

NAVEL CENTER: SELF AND OTHER

The navel center determines the amount of sexual energy available to you. When open, this energy center facilitates the giving and receiving of pleasure, but when blocked, this center can cause inability to orgasm, premature orgasm, or impotence. Issues related to the navel center are desire and pleasure, recreative sexuality, consciousness of creativity, and flexibility or resilience. When this center is balanced, you gain equal pleasure both from giving and from receiving, and you are able to understand the role of sexuality in your relationships. When the navel center is dominated by the star-tide, you may be selfish or arrogant. When this center is dominated by the earth-tide, you may start to feel insecure, mistrustful of others, and overly concerned with how others see you.

Connecting your navel center to your partner's intensifies the pleasure experienced during sex, helps to increase feelings of satisfaction with your partner, strengthens your desire to give your partner pleasure, stimulates creativity, and increases desire.

Orange is considered to be the color of the navel center in the West. This center can be activated through the herbs coriander, gokshura, marshmallow root, and uva ursi.[4] The state of your navel center determines your ability to express Goat consciousness.

SOLAR PLEXUS CENTER: EVALUATION AND JUDGMENT

A balanced solar plexus center helps you to be self-sufficient and independent, setting your own standards and striving to meet them. When this center is dominated by the star-tide, you may tend to be extremely critical of others, judging them harshly or unfairly. When this center is dominated by the earth-tide, you may find yourself seeking approval from others or trying to prove your worth by meeting others' standards.

Making a connection between your solar plexus center and your partner's can increase empathy between you, eliminate manipulativeness, remove the tendency to see sex as a commodity or a bargaining chip, and increase vitality.

Western metaphysics assigns the color yellow to the solar plexus. Herbs that stimulate this energy center include black pepper, cayenne, cumin, and goldenseal.[5] The state of your solar plexus center determines your ability to express Earth Mother consciousness.

HEART CENTER: EMOTIONS AND RELATIONSHIPS

The heart center is associated with love and friendship. A heart center that is dominated by the star-tide contributes to jealousy, possessiveness, and other manipulative behaviors designed to control others through their emotions. A heart center that is dominated by the earth-

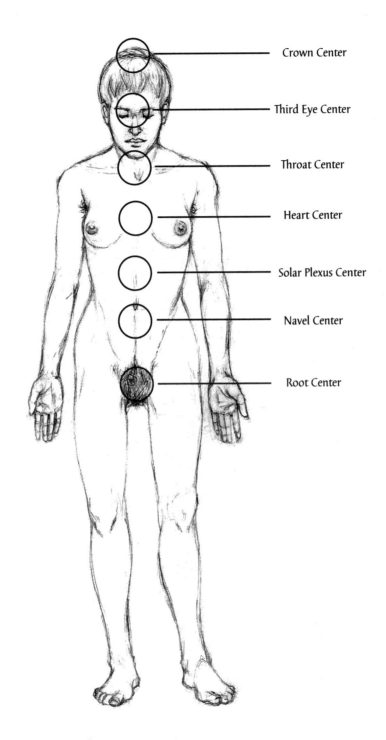

Crown Center

Third Eye Center

Throat Center

Heart Center

Solar Plexus Center

Navel Center

Root Center

The Seven Energy Centers

73

tide can increase feelings of insecurity, encouraging tendencies toward self-doubt or self-punishment. When this center is balanced, you are able to love others as well as yourself.

When your heart center is connected to your partner's, you will find it easier to merge with your partner energetically. It will also strengthen the emotional bonds between you and increase your sense of self-worth.

The color of the heart center is green. Cardamom, lotus seeds, rose and saffron activate this center.[6] The state of your heart center determines your ability to express Sky Father consciousness.

THROAT CENTER: COMMUNICATION AND PURIFICATION

A balanced throat center allows you to communicate clearly with your partner, trusting them to listen to what you are saying and to take it seriously. When your throat center is dominated by the star-tide, you may find yourself being domineering, trying to control others by imposing your ideals on them. When your throat center is dominated by the earth-tide you may tend to be submissive, and may try to manipulate others through displays of weakness.

A connection between your throat center and your partner's will make it easier for you to communicate with your partner and help you to "clear the air" of any negative emotions either of you may be holding in.

The throat center is designated as light blue, and is affected by ajwan, bayberry, cloves and licorice.[7] The state of your throat center determines your ability to express Star consciousness.

THIRD EYE CENTER: PERCEPTION AND UNDERSTANDING

The third eye center is concerned with issues of perception, insight, and wisdom. Activation of the third eye may enhance your intuition and help you to sense energy more clearly. When your third eye center is dominated by the star-tide, anxiousness, oversensitivity, and a tendency to blow things out of proportion may result. When this center is dominated by the earth-tide, you may experience suppression of fear, insensitivity to your environment, or a desire not to question the status quo.

The connection of your third eye center with your partner's can induce a merging of consciousnesses. It has the poential to increase your intuitive understanding of your partner, and open the way for spontaneous connection with the divine.

Indigo, a dark purplish blue, is associated with the third eye center. Herbs that activate the third eye center are basil, elecampane, mugwort, sandalwood, and skullcap.[8] The state of your third eye center determines your ability to express Moon God consciousness.

CROWN CENTER: BLISS AND EXPERIENCE OF UNITY

The crown center is not really a chakra, but is an energetic opening through which energy can enter and leave the body. The crown is our link to the collective consciousness, to the Divine awarenes sought in the practice of sacred sexuality. Working with the crown center can help you understand your place in the universe. When balanced, this center is your link to the collective consciousness. A crown center dominated by the star-tide makes it difficult for you to live in consensus reality, and can result in a tendency to immerse yourself in spiritual pursuits without ever applying your spiritual knowledge to your life. When this center is dominated by the earth-tide, denial of spirituality and of the spiritual self and an inability to sense anything beyond the rational, everyday conception of the self are common.

A connection between your crown center and your partner's increases feelings of bliss, allows for complete merging on the level of consciousness, and leaves you open to the experience of the unity state.

The crown center is depicted as violet (a light purple) in the West. Calamus, gotu kola, nutmeg and valerian stimulate this energy center.[9]

Balancing the Energy Centers

Do the exercises described above for strengthening the earth-tide and the star-tide, but as you bring the energy up and/or down, imagine that when it reaches each energy center, that center lights up and begins to glow.

Cleansing the Energy Centers

This is a meditation for cleaning out and revitalizing each of the energy centers. It can be done alone or with a partner. We've described this exercise as performed with the root center, but it can be done with each of the centers in turn, while visualizing the appropriate color.

If you are doing this exercise by yourself, sit in a comfortable position, keeping your spine straight and your hands placed palms-down against your thighs. Focus on your root center, visualizing it as a small red sphere of light. As you inhale, imagine energy coming into your root center through your back. As the energy enters the center, the center expands slightly and glows a little more brightly. As you exhale, the energy center begins to spin. With each complete breath, the energy center gets a little bit bigger, a little bit brighter, and begins to spin a little more.

Keep expanding the center until it is about the size of a grapefruit (although this size can vary depending on your needs at the time) and is glowing a fiery red. As it glows and spins, it burns away impurities, stagnant energy, and any negativity that may be present.

When you are ready to quit, place your palms flat on the ground and let any excess energy flow into the earth. This is important, and you should do this even if it seems somewhat absurd. As the energy flows out of your body, the energy center that has been charged will slowly return to its normal size.

To do this exercise with a partner, sit facing your partner, palms together. Once you have both expanded your energy centers completely, you can begin passing energy back and forth between your two centers. Draw the energy from your root center up your spine, down your right arm, and out through your right palm. Your partner receives this energy through the left palm, and draws it down to his or her root center.

At the same time, your partner should draw energy from the root, bringing it up the spine and pushing it down the right arm and out through the right palm. You receive this energy through your left palm, draw it up your left arm and down into your root center. Together, you and your partner form a complete circuit, passing energy from your energy center to his or hers, and then back again to yours.

As the energy moves back and forth, it will build. You may experience a vibration or buzzing sensation throughout your body while doing this; don't panic, this is normal. If it becomes too uncomfortable or intense, feel free to break the circuit and end this exercise by grounding. If you don't feel anything, or if only one person feels something, don't stop. The flow is actually occurring spontaneously—you simply need to develop your sensitivity until you are aware of it.

When you are ready to quit, separate your palms from your partner's and place them flat on the ground, allowing any excess energy to flow into the earth.

ATTITUDE

All of the exercises in this book should be tried in the spirit of exploration. As you become familiar with them, you will start to realize instinctively how each one can help you deal with various imbalances. This will allow you to develop the ability to influence your moods and states of consciousness. This ability gives you a certain spiritual resilience that will help you to explore various states of consciousness without getting stuck in them. In other words, these exercises give you greater control over the wavelength of consciousness you are tuned in to. As you become more skilled at choosing which consciousness state you exist in, you will discover other tricks or techniques that make the process of switching easier for you. You know best what you need to do, so don't hesitate to modify these techniques as needed.

ENDNOTES

1. There are exceptions. However, don't assume you are one of them without first understanding the section on Shadows in this chapter. Even if you favor a particular tide, this doesn't mean it is your strongest tide.

2. For an excellent workbook on the Eastern view of chakras and how to work with them, try Dr. Jonn Mumford's *A Chakra and Kundalini Workbook: Psychospiritual Techniques for Health, Rejuvenation, Psychic Powers and Spiritual Realization.* For an outstanding overview of the Western system of chakras, there is Anodea Judith's *Wheels of Light,* which, in addition to having many helpful visualizations, includes a detailed list of magical correspondences for each chakra.

3. *The Yoga of Herbs: An Ayurvedic Guide to Herbal Medicine,* Dr. David Frawley and Dr. Vasant Lad. Lotus Light, 1986.

4. Ibid.

5. Ibid.

6. Ibid.

7. Ibid.

8. Ibid.

9. Ibid.

FIVE

Balance, Gender Roles, and Sexual Warfare

The system we are describing in this book is based on the Sexual Mysteries of ancient cultures that were transitioning between two very different ways of life, and on the polarities that arose from the gender roles existing during that time.

Some people may object to basing a spiritual path on this polarity. Their objections are understandable in light of the past treatment of both women and men in various societies. Too often, the biological differences between men and women have been used as an excuse for mistreatment of one gender or the other. This abuse rests on the assumption that "equality" means "sameness"—that in order for two things to be deserving of equal treatment, they must be identical. From this false assumption comes the conclusion that, because the sexes are different, one of them must be superior to the other.

When these mysteries were first practiced, biology and gender were inseparable in the minds of the participants. They believed that men were one way and that women were another, and that these polar modes of existence were a function of one's physical sex. When the various systems of energy movement (Indian, Chinese, Japanese) were first developed, they were described by people existing in a cultural environment of rigid gender roles, and they reflect the biases of this environment. These rigid gender roles were largely influenced both by biological imperatives and social conditions.

Today, we are more flexible about gender roles. Many people no longer allow themselves to be confined to a role that is determined by their biological sex. However, the basic polarities—that of the Goat and the Star—are still useful today. They are energy configurations that can help us to connect, through cooperation, with the divine. The male body tends to run energy downward, and the female body tends to run energy upward; cultural and biological imperatives reinforce this pattern. However, men can learn to run energy upward, and women can learn to run energy downward. Some people do this already. Both of these polarities exist within each of us, but one will usually be stronger than the other.

In truth, the differences between men and women are to be celebrated, for it is difference that allows polarity to exist. From polarity arises life, and all the beauty that surrounds us. Without polarity, there would be no passion, no creative force, no love. The difference between maleness and femaleness is the source of the mysteries. When the energies of opposite polarity come together with awareness, they form a circuit through which Divine Consciousness can flow.

THE IMPORTANCE OF BALANCE

Each form of consciousness—the terrestrial and the celestial—has its own strengths and weaknesses, and each complements the other. In order to be whole, a person must have access to both forms of consciousness. This balance can be achieved within a person, and also between people. The Sexual Mysteries are a way to create a balance between two individuals, which will then be mirrored in the consciousness of each individual.

CREATIVITY AS A BALANCING FORCE

The flow of energy within your body is highly dynamic, and adapts to the situation at hand. This adaptability is very important, as it allows you to cycle between different states of consciousness and to be very creative. If you were stuck in one state of consciousness, you would become creatively blocked. Without the sky-tide, there are no dreams or ideas; without the earth-tide, there is no manifestation—nothing to make an idea work in a practical sense. The completion of any creative endeavor is an indication that both tides have been channeled into the effort successfully. Conversely, the need to be creative encourages you to achieve a balanced state of consciousness.

Imagine yourself as the driver of a chariot pulled by two horses (one for each tide). How fast and far the chariot goes is dependent not only on how strong the horses are, but on how well they are matched. If one horse is stronger, the chariot will tend to go off the road. If the horses are very mismatched, the chariot could actually go in circles! In order to stay the course, you, as the driver, must continually rein in the strong horse and/or crack the whip over the weaker one. Alternately, you could stop every so often, swap the positions of the horses, and continue. There are two lessons we can get from this analogy. First, balance is important to arrive at your goals. Second, there are some kinds of balance that are more elegant and efficient than others.

OUTER BALANCE

Most people habitually favor one form of consciousness over another. The more strongly you do this, the more difficult it will be for you to be creative. If you are working alone, your most difficult task is to channel your weaker tide. A sky-dominant artist might have an inspiration for a towering sculpture, but may not be able to find the right materials to craft it from, or may have to compromise the ideal form of the work with the influences of gravity and/or available funds. An earth-dominant empathic healer may encounter a patient with a strange illness that resists usual treatments, and may need to struggle to understand it well enough to devise a new treatment. However, a person may recognize their imbalance and can seek out and work with someone who can complement them energetically. Thus, the artist can find a patron who can support the project. The healer can discuss the patient with someone of a more theoretical frame of mind.

A different situation is encountered when you are working on a creative task with someone who is energetically similar to you. Progress will be extremely difficult unless one of you shifts the flow of your energy to complement that of the other. This type of partnership offers a chance to learn new ways of running your energy.

INNER BALANCE

Working on a creative task with another person who complements you energetically is not only a wonderful way to achieve a goal, but is also an opportunity to learn how to run your energy in a new way by observing the other person. This idea of working with another person to achieve a balanced state of consciousness is fundamental to the Sexual Mysteries. The intimacy of a sexual relationship breaks down barriers of self between two people in a way rarely achieved elsewhere. The merging of a person with his or her energetic opposite teaches each an enormous amount, and creates an inner balance that reflects the outer balance.

Using a creative goal to achieve a balanced state of consciousness with someone who is energetically similar to you is also fundamental to the Sexual Mysteries. The sexual relationship (the creative goal, in this case) creates a strong desire for complementation, and so having a sexual relationship with someone who is energetically similar will cause one partner to shift their internal tides to accommodate the other person and make the relationship work. This also creates an inner balance, which is then reflected in an outer balance.

BALANCE AND THE ARCHETYPES

Expression of the six archetypes described in Chapter Three may be found in everyone to a greater or lesser extent. If a person noticeably expresses an archetype, this archetype is referred to as an aspect of the person's personality. Deities, too, are often depicted as having more than one aspect. For example, Zeus is seen as both a Sky Father (in his role as stern patriarch leader) and as a Goat (in his lustful exploits).

Three of the archetypes are celestial, and three are terrestrial. Three are male, and three are female. Each archetype is balanced either by its sexual opposite or its energetic opposite. When an archetype is balanced in an inner or an outer way, the expression of that archetype is of a beneficial nature. When the archetype is not balanced, the expression is unpleasant, harsh or weak. As mentioned above, the balanced pair of the Great Mother and the Moon God are not strongly relevant to the Sexual Mysteries described in this book, and will not be discussed here in great detail. However, it should be noted that two people who have these as principal aspects of their personality may have difficulties in pursuing these Sexual Mysteries, and should either try to emphasize other aspects of themselves or find partners who can help bring out these other aspects.

From mythology, we can derive descriptions of the archetypes from the deities who expressed them in both balanced and imbalanced states.

THE GOAT

This archetype is youthful, vigorous, powerful, and deeply connected with the rhythms of the earth. He is a lord of plants and animals, of shepherds and hunters, of life and death. He is strong, quick, agile, reactive, living in the moment. He is focused on the satiation of physical desire. The Goat is willingly ruled by instinctive drives, for he knows that instinct is a finely crafted thing that must be trusted. The idea of suppressing emotions and instincts is appalling to him.

The Goat's connection with the earth does not in any way make him dull or plodding. His intelligence is the intelligence of earth—he is

cunning, thinks quickly on his feet, and can be devious if he thinks it will help him. The Goat has no interest in abstractions, but prefers to deal with tangibles. Rather than using his intelligence to avoid consequences by planning ahead, the Goat relies on his wit to keep him one step ahead of trouble. The Goat is the enemy of pretense, and gladly uses his sense of humor to bring the more celestial archetypes back down to earth. He is a self-aware animal, just like all humans, but he has looked into the face of his animal nature and embraced it. The Goat sees himself as being an integral part of the physical world.

The Goat's emotions are strong, and he has difficulty hiding them. He seeks instant gratification, and is uninterested in setting long-term goals for himself. He lives completely in the present. The Goat's sexuality is very sensual and very primal, and he has sex as often as he can, for no other reason than that it feels good. He has no ulterior motives, and the idea of emotional commitment is foreign to him.

When in balance, he is strong, smart, instinctive, amorous, passionate, funny, practical, and physically talented. He can also be a lot of fun at parties.

The Goat is destructive when he is not balanced, and may act violently without considering the consequences of his actions. He is impatient and gets wildly angry when confronted with barriers. He is easily frustrated with abstractions, and unwilling to put in the commitment necessary for achieving long-term goals. The imbalanced Goat is emotionally uncontrolled, sexually irresponsible, selfish, sometimes physically dangerous, sullen, childish, moody, and bestial.

THE STAR

Also known as the Celestial Goddess or Celestial Virgin, she is a beacon of wisdom and civilization. She is the source of inspiration and insight, the bringer of revelation. She sees herself as a part of the physical world, but is moved by forces that transcend the realm of matter.

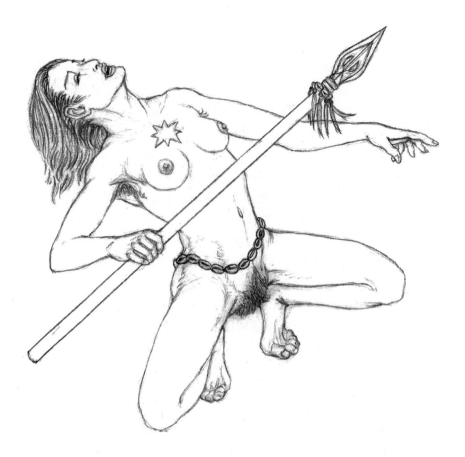

The Star is independent and self-reliant, and takes great pride in her skills. She cannot be controlled directly, but her lack of emotional restraint can be used against her. Her emotions filter through her intellect, and she loves to play games on the emotional level. Because emotions seem like abstractions to her, the Star has no compunctions about manipulating them. To the Star, the symbol is more important than the thing it represents. She does not set long-term goals for herself, but pursues ideals.

She is not chaste, but merely "unmarried." Her sexuality, like the rest of her, resists emotional entanglement and cannot be controlled by her lovers or her family members. The Star is sensual, but is focused on the emotions that arise during sex rather than the physical sensations that produce them. Sex is symbolic to the Star, and serves as a measure of her attractiveness and her worth. As the force behind civilization, she is not only concerned with seduction (the means of bringing men into civilization), but also with war (the means by which civilization expands and survives). She sees her sexual prowess (like her prowess on the battlefield) as a direct reflection of her worth as an individual, and she loves all forms of competition. The Star is reflected in the joy a woman feels when she knows that a lover desires her. The Star is also reflected in the celebratory feeling of release that comes from defeating an enemy (the "war-gasm"). Because of her celestial, abstract viewpoint, the Star is able to glory equally in conquering a heart or conquering a foe. From her lofty vantage, these are essentially the same.

When in balance, the Star brings inspiration and perspective. She is clever, humorous, and witty. She is able to apply her intellect to her relationships, and takes joyful pride in figuring out how to best please her lovers. She is able to see the bigger picture, and to act in small and subtle ways that eventually have potent effects. She chooses her battles and her lovers well.

When the Star is not balanced, she becomes ruthless and will set destructive plans into action. She becomes impatient with physical limitations, and she engages in unnecessary conflicts. She also has little respect for the emotions of others and will manipulate them to achieve her goals. The Star has no compunctions about putting people through tests to determine their worth. Because she doesn't always understand emotions, she may inflame them to the point of pain. Sometimes the imbalanced Star simply retreats from reality into her own fantasy world.

THE SKY FATHER

Like the Star, the Sky Father is celestial in nature. Mythologically, he is often linked with lightning and with mountains. The Sky Father is the organizational force behind civilization. He is a leader, a thinker, a maker of rules and laws, and is concerned with the creation of social roles and the preservation of social harmony. He is proud of his logical intellect and his ability to detect patterns and trends.

Like the Star, he is an archetype of war. But where warfare is an art to the Star, the Sky Father has it down to a science. Both the Star and the Sky Father are willing to fight for abstract ideals, and to defer short-term pleasure in order to achieve long-term goals. However, unlike the Star, the Sky Father sees his emotions as distractions that prevent him from carrying out his plans.

To the Sky Father, sexuality is a little mysterious and sometimes frightening. He may fear that his intellect will be incapacitated by the

passion that sex calls up in him, or he may be afraid that his partner will use sex to emotionally enslave him. On a positive level, sex can be cathartic and motivational for him, offering him a means of emotional expression and a reason to achieve intellectually. His awareness of the reproductive potential of sex (and the responsibilities that accompany reproduction) drives the Sky Father to be a provider and a protector.

When in balance, the Sky Father is a great teacher, a caring father, and a guardian who is willing to sacrifice himself, when necessary, for the good of his charges. He is a judge who oversees and enforces the keeping of promises. He is a keen observer, and revels in organized and analytical thought. He is particularly fond of disciplines such as science, logic, philosophy, martial arts, and mathematics. He exercises restraint in conflict, but is willing to fight for what is right.

The unbalanced Sky Father is a harsh leader and a teacher of cruel lessons. He can be jealous, possessive and suspicious, and is prone to playing "mind games" with people. He has little regard for individuals' lives and emotions, and may be (like the unbalanced Star) ruthless, manipulative and domineering. The rules he makes will be self-serving, rather than benefitting the greater good—and he will break them when it suits his purpose, because he understands how arbitrary they are, in spite of the fact that he may present them to others as natural law. He is also prone to creating complicated, abstract conceptual systems that have no practical application. When his ability to unite with the Earth Mother is denied him, he will go to war for petty reasons, seeking the thrill of victory (war-gasm).

The Sky Father does not have a particularly good reputation these days, because the Judeo-Christian and Islamic religious traditions worship gods that embody this archetype in a very unbalanced way. The modern Sky Father has been denied the balance of a relationship with an Earth Mother. The Judeo-Christian and Islamic religious traditions deny the existence of feminine divinity and devalue men's interactions with women. Unfortunately, this imbalanced manifestation of the Sky Father comprises the sum total of most Westerns' understanding of the Divine.

The Earth Mother

Like the Goat, the Earth Mother is potent, strong and fertile, and is associated with rivers, rich soil, burgeoning forests and womb-like caves deep within the earth. She is a nurturer and caretaker, and she brings all things into being in this world. Her love can be felt as an almost palpable force, gentle and warm. However, if her children or her creations are threatened, she can fight as ferociously as a mother bear defending her cubs. She is able to smooth the rough spots from transitions in life, and to soothe inflamed emotions. She is able to strengthen family or group bonds. The Earth Mother is practical, intelligent, and empathic, and is willing to aid those in need if they are willing to accept her help. Her love is sensual, passionate and earthy. The Earth Mother's strength is in her ability to sustain those things she loves.

The gentle stroking of a lover's brow after making love or the soft kiss upon the forehead of a sleeping child are both expressions of Earth Mother energy. The Earth Mother understands the power of touch to heal and to connect. She is the weaver of the emotional bonds that hold all people together. The Earth Mother is the binding force of civilization, encouraging social ties, emotional networking, and the strengthening of relationships between people. Foremost in her mind is the common good, and the Earth Mother embodies creative manifestation in practical, tangible ways which benefit her and her loved ones.

The Earth Mother's sexuality is based on emotions. Sex, for her, is not only an act of pleasure but is also an expression of love and commitment. She understands the creative power of sex, both physically and mentally, and she uses it as a means of stimulating her creativity.

Unfortunately, the Earth Mother is strongly devalued in modern times, to such an extent that even women do not respect this aspect in themselves, and choose to limit their creative power due to lack of self-esteem and fear of ridicule.

In balance, the Earth Mother creates a foundation from which all things may flourish. She teaches us how to love and how to be loved. She holds families and other groups together. The Earth Mother teaches

us how to respect emotions, and is quick to gently but firmly correct actions that cause pain to others. She can put ideas into practice, and, when inspired, is capable of awesome feats of creative self-expression.

When she is out of balance, the Earth Mother can be smothering, and may make it difficult for her loved ones to be independent. She will be unhappy with the idea of losing her emotional control over others, and may use guilt or other forms of manipulation to ensure what she sees as "proper behavior." The imbalanced Earth Mother may selectively withdraw her love as a passive sort of punishment when she is upset with someone, or when she is not getting her way. She can also be prone to giving away her creativity, using it solely to support the goals of others.

ARCHETYPAL RELATIONSHIPS

Now that we have described the archetypes in both their balanced and imbalanced manifestations, it should be easy for you to begin seeing some of these in your own personality. But what is the significance of this? What does it mean if you tend to be a Sky Father, or a Goat? Is it better to be an Earth Mother than a Star?

No archetype is better than any other. In fact, one of the aims of the Sexual Mysteries is to be able to experience multiple forms of consciousness. The mysteries are a means of bringing together complementary forms of consciousness, using the sex act as a catalyst, to achieve unity states of consciousness. In a unity state, two complementary consciousnesses are joined synergistically to create a third form of consciousness (Figure 5.1).

According to the mysteries, terrestrial consciousness joins with celestial consciousness. Consciousness constantly and continuously divides itself in half and then rejoins those halves. With each split, the halves acquire new information and experiences which are not available to the other half. With each joining, these halves share their new understandings by re-fusing with each other. This process, which may be thought of as a reproductive cycle for consciousness, is the means by which consciousness evolves (refer back to Figure 3.2). Sacred sex is sacred because it makes the world-spirit whole again, allowing it to awaken. It rejoins matter and spirit, reenacting the union that created all things.

Because each cycle of division and reunion is a step in evolution, these cycles are reflected in quantum changes in human nature. The transition from pre-tribal to tribal consciousness, for instance, was catalyzed by the successful fusion of the consciousnesses of the Great Mother and the Moon God. The fusion of the Goat and Star made possible the beginning of human civilization. We suspect that the fusion of the Earth Mother and the Sky Father will give humans access to two new archetypes and will facilitate a type of life that will be so fundamentally different that all of our present imaginings cannot possibly

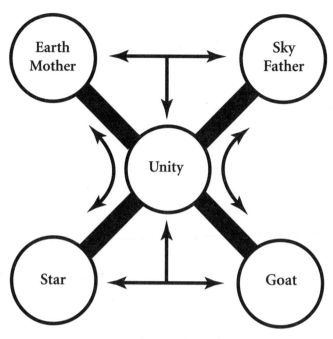

Figure 5.1: Balancing the Archetypes

encompass it. As more humans achieve balanced states of consciousness, the Earth Mother/Sky Father fusion will become stronger, allowing the next quantum shift in human nature to occur.

It is possible to achieve simultaneous pairings of consciousness, such as a mixture of Goat/Sky Father consciousness, or Star/Earth Mother consciousness. It is also quite possible to remain in the unity state, without immediately moving to one of the more polarized states. With practice, this will begin happening spontaneously. Keep in mind that while sometimes you are "changing channels" between archetypes, it is also possible to widen your bandwidth of consciousness as well.

CONSCIOUSNESS SHIFTS

During lovemaking, there is a dynamic interplay between the archetypes that each partner is expressing. There is a tendency for one or both partners to be influenced by each other to shift their consciousness. Of course, people are free to resist this influence, and sometimes do so out of fear of exploring their shadow side. Overcoming this fear is of great importance in the Sexual Mysteries.

One type of shift is a complementary shift. If one partner is expressing the Goat archetype, his partner may find herself expressing the Star. The Sky Father in one partner may bring out the Earth Mother in the other. Sex between complementary archetypes is mysterious, erotic, passionate, and intriguing. The other type of shift is an attunement shift. If one partner is expressing a celestial archetype, the other person may begin doing so as well. This holds true for terrestrial archetypes as well. Sex between energetically attuned archetypes is reassuring, friendly, and playful.

During foreplay and sex, a unity state can be achieved between two people. The two together create a greater whole. This may be experienced in a variety of ways, ranging from a deep sense of intimacy to a profound spiritual merging and temporary loss of individual identity. This state of unity may ebb and flow, and should not be thought of as something that only happens at the climax of a session (although climax is often associated with the more profound types of merging).

As people experience unity, they begin to influence each other, and shifts in consciousness occur. The exercises in this book are designed to increase your ability to "let go" and allow these shifts to happen, as well as to make conscious decisions to shift between archetypes. As your ability to shift improves, the transitions between archetypes will become more fluid and less perceptible. As this happens, the archetypes merge, and you will find yourself expressing them simultaneously. Ideally, each person achieves this state and shares it, through lovemaking, with their partner. The man, as the merged Goat/Sky Father, joins with the woman, as the merged Star/Earth Mother, and together become a divinely creative, supremely aware whole. The sex is simultaneously playful and erotic, mysterious and reassuring, passionate and friendly. Even coming close to this is wonderful, so don't become obsessed with attaining this ideal state. Enjoy what you achieve, and recognize that it is worthwhile. Sometimes you may not be emotionally or mentally prepared for such a profound experience, and may decide to limit your expression of consciousness (e.g. just act like a Goat or Star). If you need to keep things simple, pay attention to that need.

SEXUAL COMPETITION

Polarity is desirable in the relationship between the sexes. Polarity creates attraction, and the release of energy that comes from joining polarities can be used to alter consciousness. However, we often make the mistake of expressing that polarity through competition. The need to compete sexually is often due to an insecurity about one's own power and a fear that the other possesses something better. Competition on this level prevents terrestrial and celestial energies from coming together in a complementary way, eliminating the possibility of achieving a unity state. In any encounter between men and women, competition means fragmentation. If one person wins, both lose.

SEXUAL BALANCE

If any of this sounds familiar, don't feel bad, because we've been describing problems that can be solved. Self-respect is crucial for preventing imbalance. If you respect your part in the mysteries, you will not wonder if someone else's part is better. You will be able to relax and welcome whatever your partner has to offer you, in an atmosphere of mutual respect. This is the most fundamental principle of the Sexual Mysteries, and everything else develops naturally from this.

Unfortunately, most of the existing systems of sacred sex were developed in cultures whose archetypes were imbalanced, where gender roles reflected the resulting imbalance of power between the sexes. This imbalance arises from insecurity, and had a powerful impact on the philosophies of ancient Tantric practitioners.

SEX, MAGICK, AND SPIRIT

One of the key factors underlying these insecurities is the equation of sexual fluids with life-force. When Eastern Tantra was first developed, its practitioners understood the connection between normal orgasm (which involves ejaculation) and energy loss. However, they did not differentiate between the energy that was lost and the ejaculated semen. As a result, they assumed that loss of sexual fluids was detrimental to the health of the male, and based their practices on the conservation of semen.

Furthermore, because women did not ejaculate, it was assumed they retained not only their own life-force, but also the energy released by the man during orgasm. Woman was seen as stealing man's energy through sex. In fact, many ancient Tantric texts warn against teaching women any of the sexual techniques described therein, because of the possibility that women would become adept at these techniques and use them to steal the life-force of their partners. This fear is the origin of the Tantric preference for virgins as sexual partners, and is also the basis for the Tantric recommendation that a man have sex with as many different women as possible, avoiding emotional attachment to any one woman.

Male Tantrists were gradually overtaken by paranoia about ejaculation. For example, one ancient Chinese text refers to the female sexual partner as "your adversary" and recommends that the man "control a woman as you would a runaway horse with a rotten rope. Be as apprehensive [of ejaculation] as you might of falling into a deep hole filled with sword points. If you love your semen, your life will be indestructible."[1] To someone who exists in this mindset, a woman's pleasure is only important because, in her ecstatic state, she produces the compounds in her vaginal fluid which were thought to grant immortality to the male who absorbs it. Woman became a resource to be exploited sexually, rather than an equal partner in ecstasy. Countless ancient texts are devoted to the ways in which women could be used for this purpose.

This paranoia is less pronounced in Indian Tantra, but reaches a fever peak in the Chinese Taoist literature, where the fear of ejaculation is compounded by the reliance on an oversimplified understanding of the yin-yang principle. In applying the yin-yang model to gender relations, ancient Chinese tantrists simplified the concepts of yin and yang, equating yang with both the male principle and with celestial energy, and equating yin with the female principle and with terrestrial energy. In doing so, they forgot that each half contains a portion of the other, and so designated man as Heaven (embodying Sky Father consciousness) and woman as Earth (embodying Earth Mother consciousness). They forgot that men can also manifest terrestrial energy (Goat consciousness) and that women can manifest celestial energy (Star consciousness).

Because there was no place for the Goat or the Star in their model of the universe, men and women were confined to a single, socially proscribed role: men were fathers, women were mothers. This model reinforced the then-current social structures of these cultures. When men and women are cut off from half of themselves, they become disempowered, and are much easier to control, both socially and politically. We suffer from similar gender problems in the West today. If the Sexual Mysteries are to be a means of resolving these problems, they must be free from the biases that created those problems.

We do not wish to denigrate Eastern spiritual systems. After all, they developed the Tantric system, and laid much of the groundwork for what we discuss in this book. The techniques of Tantra are invaluable for anyone wishing to explore the interface between body and mind. However, many of the cultural assumptions of ancient Tantrists were transferred to their spiritual teachings. These gender biases are inappropriate for us today, and we would like to remove from sacred sexuality those cultural biases that interfere with our ability to achieve an integrated state of consciousness.

As Tantra has been imported into the Western world, it has been modified slightly for the Western mindset. Unfortunately, it still retains many of the same elements that reinforced its original gender imbalance. We continue to re-create the mistakes of the past, rather than learning from them. In *Sexual Energy Ecstasy*, David Ramsdale describes an encounter with a modern-day practitioner who was using her

Tantric abilities to steal energy from her sexual partners.[2] Gavin and Yvonne Frost, in their book *Tantric Yoga*, observe that as practitioners become more experienced in Tantric practice, they "begin to play games with each other, trying to make the other have an orgasm while refraining themselves."[3] Unfortunately, the Frosts do not recognize this phenomenon as an indication of a fundamental problem in the way that Tantra is often taught. They see this type of sexual competition as normal. It is clear that there are still those who have not escaped the tendency in Eastern Tantra towards sexual vampirism, and are still struggling with the same insecurities that ancient Tantric students experienced.

If we could communicate only one thing to you, it would be this: Cooperation is the way to achieve balance between the sexes. Cooperation leads to the unity state; competition ultimately leads to fragmentation of consciousness. The single most effective tool we have for restoring a balance between the sexes is our willingness to help each other—to share our experiences, to share our understanding, to share our love, to share ourselves.

ENDNOTES

1. *The Tao of Sex: The Essence of Medical Prescriptions (Ishimpo)*, Howard S. Levy and Akira Ishihara.
2. *Sexual Energy Ecstasy: A Practical Guide to Lovemaking Secrets of the East and West*, David and Ellen Ramsdale, p. 79. Peak Skill Publishing, 1991.
3. *Tantric Yoga: The Royal Path to Raising Kundalini Power*, Gavin and Yvonne Frost. Samuel Weiser, Inc., 1989.

SIX

Preparatory Exercises

S atori. Revelation. Epiphany. Ecstasy. Enlightenment. Everybody wants to experience this state of mind. But what is it? The enlightenment experience is a realization that allows you to gain a completely new perspective on your current reality. Most people see enlightenment as an ending point—an apex—and think that once you've achieved it, you'll be able to stay in this state of mind for the rest of your life. They are often quite disappointed to find that, after a short period of time, this state of mind fades and they return to the mundane world. Many people, having experienced this initial ecstatic state of mind, spend the rest of their lives trying to return to it—and begin to doubt whatever understanding they might have gained from the experience.

However, their disappointment is rooted in a misunderstanding of the nature of revelation. Enlightenment is not a state in which you should attempt to live, any more than you should attempt to spend the rest of your life in third grade just because you learned some really important things there. Revelation is a perspective change. It's like climbing up to a mountain to see the lay of the land below. When you have seen the view from above, it's time to come back down the mountain, and use what you've seen to improve your life. If you fail to apply the lesson of your revelation to your problems, then it's a lesson you haven't really learned.

ENLIGHTENMENT AND ORGANIZED RELIGION

The enlightenment experience is the basis of organized religion. One person (such as Buddha, Jesus, or Mohammed) experiences a sudden perspective shift which allows them to commune with divinity. This individual revelation is later formalized so that its wisdom can be accessed by people who have not had the same shift of perspective, and thus do not have the same understanding. Unfortunately, this means that one person's revelation has to be put into words, which are inadequate to convey an enlightenment experience—and in the translation, meaning is invariably lost. Organized religion is an attempt to relive another person's revelation vicariously, through language and ritual.

Most organized religions are built around a single revelation, or a series of very similar such experiences. For this reason, many people are under the misapprehension that theirs is the only truth. This is a natural mistake. After all, each religion is going to claim that its lesson is the most important one. Most organized religions encourage their members to have faith in one particular revelation rather than allowing those members to experiment on their own, and possibly experience a revelation of a different type.

Because we have been encouraged to think this way by religion, many Westerners do not realize that you can have more than one enlightenment experience. In fact, if you are growing spiritually, you will have many more. It's all right for today's revelation to differ from, or even to contradict, yesterday's. You shouldn't try to "return" to a particular revelation. Simply use what you learned there, and be ready for the next one.

A true spiritual discipline should not simply hand you someone else's revelation and ask you to believe in it. A good spiritual path is one that creates circumstances around you that will trigger these jumps of understanding within you. Many of the existing disciplines that attempt to induce revelation are based on the principle of asceticism—the idea that you must withdraw from the mundane world and focus on the divine until you have completely transcended the physical plane. These disciplines have highly developed techniques for inducing the enlightenment experience in students. However, because of these disciplines' emphasis on withdrawal from the mundane world, many students are unable to apply their experiences when they return to mundane life. Because the ascetic traditions have a high visibility in the West, many of us mistakenly believe that the only way to achieve any sort of enlightened understanding is to adopt the ascetic path. This is not true, for we have the option of following the sensual path, in which revelation is seen as coming through participation in the physical plane. The Sexual Mysteries are a sensual path, and many of the exercises described in this chapter are designed to help you create circumstances in your life which will lead you to your own revelations.

FOOD AND CONSCIOUSNESS

The food that you eat can have a tremendous impact on your consciousness, and for this reason, many spiritual disciplines include special dietary restrictions designed to prepare you for energy work and meditation. This is fine for an ascetic, who is attempting to escape his or her body, but it's not necessary for someone who is following a sensual path. The most important thing is to simply take good care of yourself. Just eat healthily, and start paying attention to the effects that different foods have on your state of mind.[1] When you eat large quantities of sugar, do you find yourself feeling depressed? When you eat foods that are high in fat, do you tend to be sluggish afterwards? Pay attention to your body, and then cut back on any foods that seem to be interfering with your ability to live well.

Many of the practices described in this book have the potential to aggravate pre-existing physical problems at first. By increasing the flow of energy through your body, you will also increase both your awareness of your physical condition and, possibly, the severity of the problem itself. You will be bringing these problems to a head so that they can be resolved (and improving your body on an energetic level *will* help to resolve them), but at the beginning you may feel more uncomfortable than normal. Use your common sense when deciding whether the uncomfortable feelings you may experience are minor or require the attention of a doctor.

We feel that health is a personal issue, and that what may be harmful to one person will be fine for another. You are the only person who can decide what is right for your body. We can only offer suggestions that have worked for us. The best way to take care of yourself is to simply observe your body, paying close attention to the ways it reacts to various situations, and then live accordingly. Your goal is not to escape your body, or to transcend it—the Sexual Mysteries are a sensual tradition. Make a temple of your body, and then invite the Divine in.

FASTING

Fasting is more suited to the ascetic traditions, but when done on a short-term basis, it can be a good way to clean toxins out of your body.

If you do choose to fast, do it at a time when there will not be many physical demands placed on your body. It is important to realize that most of the severe dietary restrictions that arose in Eastern spiritual traditions were designed for monks who spent most of their waking hours separated from the stresses of mundane life, sitting still and focusing on their internal condition. Most of us do not have that luxury, and must balance our spiritual practices against our mundane responsibilities.

When fasting, be sure to drink lots of water, and pay close attention to your physical condition. There is a difference between fasting and starving yourself, and you don't need to deprive your body of fuel for several days at a time. For some people, skipping lunch will be enough of a fast to clean out their bodies; others may want to do it for a day or two. The only way you will know the right length of time for you is to pay attention to your body. If you start having difficulty functioning mentally, or start feeling depressed, stop.

DRUGS

It is a good idea to avoid using stimulants, such as caffeine or nicotine, especially right before a session of energy work. Both caffeine and nicotine have been shown to negatively affect sexual performance. They can irritate the prostate, which increases a man's need to ejaculate. They also make it more difficult for you to achieve a state of internal awareness, because they increase your sensitivity to external stimuli. In the long term, stimulants are detrimental to your overall health. They increase your energy by forcing your glands and other tissues to work overtime. When your glands are finally exhausted, your energy level drops much lower than it would normally, and your body requires a much longer time to recuperate. Herbal stimulants, such as *ma huang* (ephedra), have the same effects: the fact that they are "natural" does not necessarily make them good for you.

We also recommend that you avoid alcohol before performing energy work. In addition to irritating the prostate, like caffeine and nicotine, alcohol also makes it more difficult for you to maintain awareness of your body—awareness that is crucial for successful energy work.

APHRODISIACS

There are a number of foods that are thought to be aphrodisiacs. Most of these foods contain nutrients (B vitamins, vitamin C, vitamin E, zinc, etc.) which not only strengthen the entire body, but also feed the reproductive system. Seeds such as sunflower, pumpkin, and sesame are excellent for strengthening sexual energy. Be careful that you do not merely rely on these foods to supplement a poor diet, though. Eating healthily is a much more effective way to increase your sexual capacity. Good health is one of the best aphrodisiacs.

We recommend that you avoid sexual stimulants like amyl nitrate (which is a carcinogen) and Spanish Fly (which irritates the urinary tract, increasing your risk of bladder infection). If you wish to try an herbal aphrodisiac, such as damiana or saffron, be certain that you research the herb thoroughly before taking it.

SETTING GOALS

Before you begin walking on a path of personal transformation, you should decide which parts of your life you wish to change and which parts you wish to keep. A good idea is to make a goal list, as shown in Figure 6.1.

Making a list like this is very important, because it not only guides you in working toward what you want, but it also reminds you of what you already have achieved. If, during the course of personal transformation, you begin to compromise the things on your "maintain" list, it is time to stop and reconsider what you are doing. Are you becoming obsessed with your spiritual growth, to the point that you are no longer able to put enough energy into keeping your job or raising your children?

CHANGE	MAINTAIN
• Become more grounded and practical • Overcome fear of intimacy • Don't fight over money • Gain more respect for the opposite sex • Quit smoking • Build self-esteem • Learn to trust intuition	• Do effective work every day • Meet financial obligations • Nurture your marriage • Exercise and diet for health • Keep your sense of humor • Sustain commitments to family and friends

Figure 6.1

If so, you may need to sit down and think about how you can meet your need for change without sacrificing the things you cherish.

RECOGNIZING YOUR DEITIES

Each person will find that they resonate strongly with particular deities. One way to discover the deities that you tune in to is to pay attention to shifts in your personality. Do you have different modes of behavior for different activities, or for dealing with different people? If you are familiar with mythology, you may see that some of your modes are very much like the behaviors of mythological figures.[2] If you are unfamiliar with mythology, you may simply try to look at your behavior and see which of the four archetypes express themselves through you, and at what times.

Most people are nervous about the idea of having more than one persona, but of course everyone does. There is no real cause for alarm unless these personas are so separate that they consider themselves independent entities, or they are fighting with each other. In a healthy psyche, the various personas are integrated and work together harmoniously—at least, most of the time.

Look at your personas—the masks you wear during different periods of your life—and analyze them. If you have trouble seeing that you have more than one personality, try the following. Take a straight-on photo of yourself, and cut it in half vertically. Place the cut edge of each half up to a mirror to create a whole face. Compare these two faces. Each face is the face of one of the dominant personas in your personality makeup. Using these faces, what can you discern about them?

Once you have examined your two dominant personas, you can get a little more detailed. Make a list of all the personas you have. Detail the one you use when dealing with the kids, the one you use in dealing with your lover, the one you use at work, etc. Write a brief description of each persona. What do they like to do? How does each of them respond to stressful situations? What are their hopes and fears? Their goals? Compare your descriptions. Do some of them overlap? Are any of them the same? Do any of them have conflicting goals? Do your personas work together, or are there times when they conflict with each other? Be honest.

Figure 6.2 gives an example of a persona analysis. After you have done your own persona analysis, look at the patterns of behavior that you find in each of your personas. In what ways are they similar to or different than the archetypes described in this book? Are there any that resemble a particular god or goddess? If you find any striking resemblances to a particular deity, chances are you are tuning in to that deity. Don't forget that women can tune in to gods, and men can tune in to goddesses. Once you have determined which deities you tune into, you have a foundation for establishing working relationships with them.

PHYSICAL PREPARATION

One way to prepare for energy work is to practice some sort of whole-body exercise. Yoga, chi gung, and martial arts are disciplines that develop many of the skills necessary for transformational sex. In addition to physical conditioning, they all develop sensitivity to and control

PERSONA #1	PERSONA #2
She is reserved, responsible, loves work that is complex and detailed. She can deal with people when she needs to, but prefers solitary pursuits (like reading). Employers love her. She never lets her personal life—or anything else—interfere with the job at hand. She can handle a tremendous workload by simply attacking it methodically and persisting until she's accomplished whatever she's set out to do. She's honest and literal-minded, and very sympathetic to the people around her. She is also a high-stress person who cares enough to worry about the problems of those around her as well as her own, and is often anxious about circumstances that are beyond her control. She has many goals and aspirations, but a lot of her dreams are not realistic. She realizes that she may never achieve these, but refuses to give up on them. She does not have many friends, but the ones she does have are quite close, and she would do anything to help them if they needed it.	She loves to surprise people, and will often go out of her way to be unpredictable. She's highly creative, very insightful, but so disorganized that she often has difficulty finishing the many projects she's started. She is interested in almost everything, but her short attention span makes it difficult for her to stick to any one thing long enough to master it. She's funny, witty, playful, and seductive—when she's in a good mood. When she's not, she can be sarcastic and unpredictable. Her companions tend to be her intellectual equals, such as fellow artists, writers, and musicians. She lives by one imperative: Avoid boredom. Everything is personal to her, and she takes everything to an extreme. She'll do anything she thinks she can get away with, provided it doesn't violate her personal sense of ethics.

Figure 6.2

of energy flow, physical and mental resilience, and good breathing technique. Additionally, many martial arts offer practice in matching a partner's energy. Martial arts that teach rolling are especially good for developing both physical and mental resilience. Belly dance is another physical discipline that will greatly enhance your sexual practice—it builds both strength and flexibility in the hips and pelvic area, while offering a safe space in which to express your sensuality.

However, you need not necessarily study exotic or esoteric physical disciplines. Other athletic activities that involve the whole body are also worthwhile: swimming, running, weight-training, aerobics—anything that does not develop your body asymmetrically (like tennis or golf)—will be beneficial, both in breaking through energy blockages and in improving your general level of health.

PREPARATORY EXERCISES

One of the primary goals of the exercises described below is to remove energy blockages and to increase the flow of energy through all parts of your body. Physical tension is indicative of energy blockage. Just as water has difficulty flowing through a hose that has been stepped on, energy has difficulty flowing through a body that is tense.

These blockages are the primary cause of the physical and mental discomfort you experience when you attempt to increase the flow of energy through your body. The greater the tension, the greater the blockage—and the greater the discomfort. If you attempt to drastically increase the energy flow through your body without first removing existing blockages, you risk depression, emotional instability, and physical illness. It is very important not to go any further with these exercises than your body and mind can handle. But even if you are cautious, you will experience both physical and emotional upset as you progress. The key to overcoming these obstacles is resilience.

Here are some simple exercises that you can do to prepare your body for the Sexual Mysteries. These exercises are all very gentle, and are to be done slowly and with awareness—awareness of the muscles contracting and expanding as you move, awareness of the bones moving in their joints, awareness of your breathing and your general body alignment. Never push your body beyond its limits—only carry out the motion until you can feel the stretch in your muscles. Many of these exercises utilize a wave-like motion. Visualizing this wave in the appropriate part of the body while you perform these exercises can be helpful. You can do as many repetitions of each exercise as you like. If you are out of shape or ill, you should start with a few repetitions, ten or fifteen, and work your way up. If you have any physical problems that might be aggravated by these exercises, consult a qualified health care practitioner before trying them.

THE CAT STRETCH

Get down on your hands and knees, hands shoulder-width apart, knees about six inches apart, back flat. Begin to curl your pelvis forward, flexing your back upward to form an arch. Do this as slowly as you can, trying to curl your back one vertebra at a time. Start from the coccyx and allow the movement to flow up your spine like a wave. Let your head hang loosely from your neck.

When you have finished this movement, begin to slowly lower your back by tilting your pelvis downward, again feeling your spine flex in the other direction one vertebra at a time, starting from the coccyx. Allow the movement to flow up your spine like a wave. When the wave of motion reaches your shoulders, raise your head—by the time the wave reaches the top of your head, you should be looking up toward the ceiling. The wavelike motion in this exercise is very important. The pelvis controls the whole motion. Do not simply arch or flex your back all at once. You can coordinate your breathing with this exercise: breathe out while you flex your back upwards, and breathe in while you flex downwards.

The Cat Stretch

HIP CIRCLES

Stand with your legs shoulder-width apart, knees slightly bent (never locked), hips loose and relaxed. Rotate your hips gently, tracing a small circle. After several repetitions (don't strain), stop, and rotate your hips in the opposite direction.

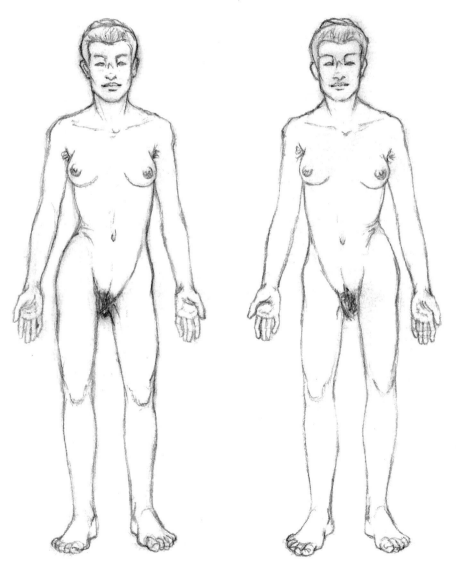

Hip Circles

BACK ARCH

Lie down on your back with your hands at your sides, palms down, and your knees bent, feet flat on the floor. Exhale and thrust your hips up towards the ceiling, holding this position for a count of five or more. Inhale, and slowly lower your back to the floor, rolling down one vertebra at a time, from the top of the neck down to the pelvis.

If you are in good shape, you can do a more advanced variation of this exercise. Do the arch with your arms over your head and the backs of your hands lying flat against the floor. If you have back problems or

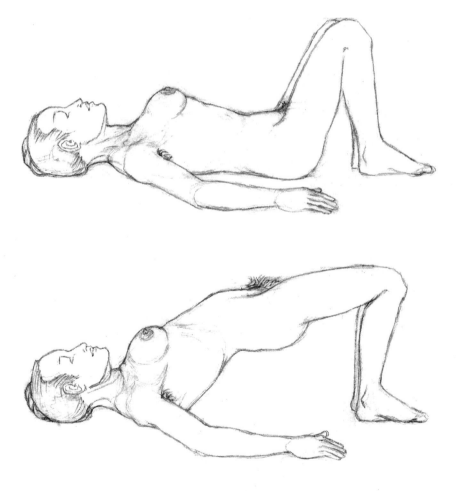

Back Arch

are out of shape, you can place your hands on the small of your back as you thrust upward, supporting your back.

PELVIC THRUSTS

Stand with your legs slightly more than shoulder width apart, knees slightly bent. Thrust your pelvis forward slowly, exhaling, then pull your pelvis back and arch your back slightly while inhaling.

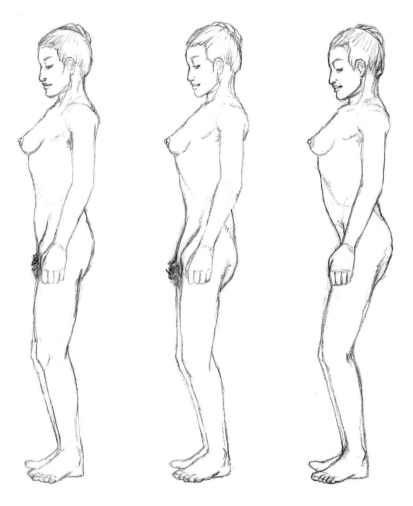

Pelvic Thrusts

RIB CAGE LIFTS

The rib cage lift is excellent for increasing both the strength and flexibility of the upper torso.

Lie flat on your back, with your arms at your sides and palms flat on the floor. (Note: if you have back problems, you might want to skip this exercise. If your back problems are minor, you can place a small pillow or rolled-up towel beneath your knees to take some of the strain off of your lower back.) Inhale, and try to lift your ribcage off the floor, keeping your shoulders, hips, and the back of your head in contact with the floor. Exhale, and return to your starting position.

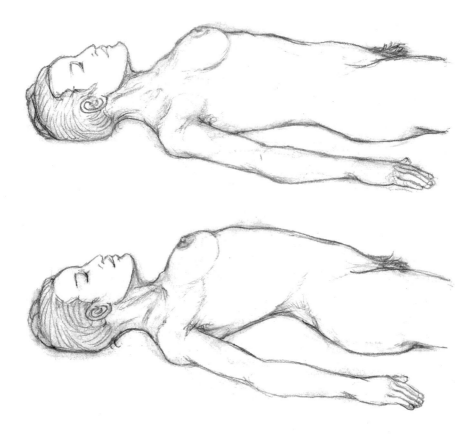

Rib Cage Lifts

UNDULATIONS

The undulation, a popular belly dance technique, is a fairly complicated movement, but well worth practicing. This can be broken into two separate motions: a rolling of the rib cage, and a flexing of the spine (the same type of flexing that occurs in the cat stretch, above). Practice these motions separately at first, then try to put them together.

To roll your ribcage, isolate the ribcage and trace a small vertical circle with your ribcage, moving your ribcage forward, then upward, then backward, then down. (If you are having difficulty with this, stand

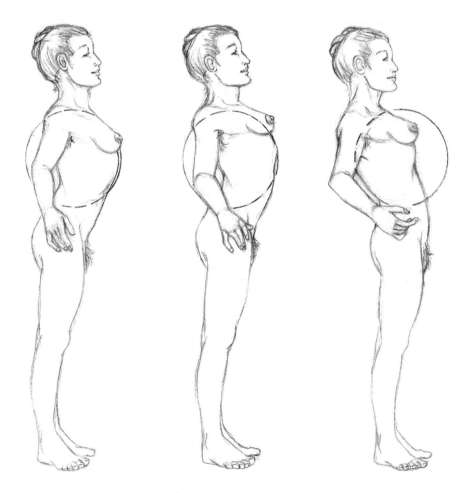

Undulations

next to a wall and imagine a circle drawn on the wall. Trace this circle with your ribcage.) These movements should eventually be blended together to form a circle, but can be practiced as four separate movements at the beginning. Do not allow your hips to move yet—keep this movement completely confined to the upper torso. Inhale during the upward and forward motions, and exhale during the downward and backward motions.

Once you have mastered the rib cage roll (and this may take a couple of weeks, so don't feel bad if you don't get it right off) you can add the rest of the movement—a gentle swaying of your hips and pelvis. As you are performing the rib cage roll, relax your pelvis, and allow the movement of the rib cage roll to flow downwards into your pelvis (again, visualize it as a wave-like motion that flows down your spine).

As you perform the upward and forward part of the roll (the first half of the circle), draw your pelvis backwards and arch your back. As you perform the backward and downward part of the roll (the second half of the circle), thrust your hips forward and flex your back. As with the cat stretch, the flexing and arching of your back should be done slowly, as if you were moving one vertebra at a time.

BELLY ROLL

The belly roll is another belly dance technique that offers outstanding sexual benefits to both men and women. To do the belly roll, stand in a comfortable position, with your feet a shoulder-width apart. Contract the muscles of your stomach, starting at the point just above your pubic bone, and allowing the contractions to flow up your stomach to the bottom of your ribcage with the same wave-like motion you practiced in the cat stretch. As each point contracts, the point before it releases.

You can also perform the belly roll in the reverse direction, rolling the abdominal muscles down from the ribcage to the top of your pubic bone.

Belly rolls increase the amount of energy in the abdominal area, which can be drawn on for magical purposes, expended in normal physical activity, or released through grounding. (Note: Your hips and ribcage do not move during this exercise—the entire movement is conducted with the stomach muscles.)

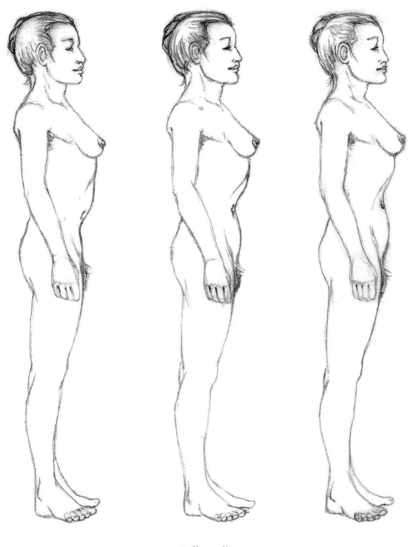

Belly Roll

Massage

Another effective method for breaking up energy blockages is deep body massage. A good massage can speed up the elimination of toxins in your body, relieve muscle tension, release stored emotions and body-memories, increase circulation of both blood and energy, and realign the misaligned portions of your body. The style of massage is less important than the approach of the massage therapist. This person is going to be manipulating your body for the purpose of changing both your physical condition and your awareness of your body, so he or she must be professional, sensitive, and responsive to your body's needs and quirks. If a massage therapist seems to be aggravating an existing physical condition or seems generally insensitive to your requests, then find another.

Of course, for many, massage therapy is a luxury—a massage can cost anywhere from $30 to $100. This does not mean that you need to rule out massage. You and your partner can learn the essentials from any good book on massage, and your local college or community center may offer inexpensive classes in which you can perfect your technique or learn more advanced strokes. If you are working alone, there are books that describe self-massage techniques.

In addition to maintaining the overall health of your body, it's also important to keep your sexual organs in good condition. Again, massage and exercise provide a foundation for sexual health. You can perform the massage yourself, or have your partner do it. Specific techniques are not nearly as important as gentleness and affection. Anal massage can also be beneficial. Not only does it help to keep the prostate gland in good condition, it has the added benefits of releasing energy through the breaking of our society's anal taboo, and of releasing many deep-rooted emotions. Be warned: Sometimes this emotional release can be so intense that the recipient of the massage will become enraged or begin to cry uncontrollably. The person giving the massage should be prepared to comfort their partner should this occur.

There are several considerations for both genital and anal massage.

- Be gentle. Never do anything that hurts, and never use any massage implements that might damage these delicate tissues. Flexible vibrators can be used, but should be a supplement to the human touch, rather than a substitute. Before you begin, make sure that your fingernails are short, and that you have no snags, jagged edges, or hangnails.

- Be clean. Before you begin, you should wash the area to be massaged with soap and water. If you are receiving an anal massage, you may also choose to clean the colon with an enema first, but this is not necessary. The person giving the massage should wash his or her hands with soap and water beforehand; and if giving both an anal and genital massage, should be sure to wash their hands after removing them from their partner's rectum.

- Use lubrication. Never use oil in vaginal massage, as it may increase the probability of bladder or vaginal infection. Water-based lubricants are best for both anal and vaginal massage, as they are not only least likely to irritate the genital tissue, but are also safe to use with latex gloves or finger-coverings.

- Be safe. If the transmission of HIV or any other sexually transmitted disease is even a slim possibility, the giver of the massage should wear latex gloves or "finger condoms" (which are now available in some drug stores).

SEXUAL EXERCISES

Exercise is also important. Keeping the pubococcygeus (PC) and surrounding muscles strong and flexible should be a priority for both men and women. Two basic sexual exercises found in Eastern Tantra are *vajroli mudra* (using PC contractions) and *aswini mudra* (using anal contractions). These contractions can be performed alone (for beginners) or in combination with breathing and meditation techniques (once you are more advanced). This exercise helps men to control ejaculation and teaches women to directly stimulate the penis during vaginal sex. It also increases the length of orgasm for both sexes.

To learn basic PC contractions (also referred to as Kegel exercises, after the doctor who made them popular in the West), try this: The next time you need to urinate, try stopping the flow of urine without flexing your legs or stomach muscles. (When men do this contraction successfully their penis should bob up and down slightly; women can insert a finger into their vagina to feel the contraction.) The muscle that you are contracting is the PC muscle.

Now that you know what these contractions feel like, you can begin to practice them. There are two ways in which you can flex this muscle—in swift, brief contractions or long, intense contractions. Start by practicing twenty-five repetitions of each type of contraction, then add a few contractions each day until you can do 100 or more of each type every day.

Once you have mastered PC contractions, you can combine them with breathing techniques. Sit cross-legged or in a chair that allows you to rest your feet flat on the floor with your thighs parallel to the ground and your spine straight. Inhale slowly and deeply, then hold your breath while performing ten PC contractions. Take a small sniff of air through your nose, then exhale slowly out the mouth. Repeat ten times. Once you are comfortable with this exercise, you can increase the number of contractions per breath and the number of repetitions

Men can also increase the strength of the PC muscle in this way: Stimulate yourself to erection, then hang a wet washcloth over your penis and perform the PC contractions. Heavier objects can be added as your PC muscles become stronger. Be sure to use common sense, and don't attach anything to your penis that might cause injury.

Women can achieve a similar effect using *ben-wa* balls—small balls made of metal or weighted latex which are inserted into the vagina. In order to keep these balls in, you must keep the PC muscle contracted (this is harder than you might think). Don't worry about losing the balls inside your vagina—the cervix is much too small to allow even one of these balls to slip through to your uterus. The only concern with ben-wa balls is keeping them from falling out and getting lost. (Hint: always remove your ben-wa balls before going to the bathroom.)

To learn to contract your anal muscles at will, the next time you need to empty your bowels, try to hold everything in for a few seconds without flexing your thigh or stomach muscles. The muscles you use to do this are the muscles that make up your anal sphincter. (If you are unsure as to whether or not your are isolating the correct muscle, insert a lubricated finger into your anus and try the exercise.) As with the PC muscle, there are two ways in which you can flex these muscles—in swift, brief contractions or long, intense contractions. Start by practicing twenty-five repetitions of each type of contraction, then add a few contractions each day until you can do 100 or more of each type every day.

Anal contractions can also be combined with breathing. Sit cross-legged (or in a chair that allows you to rest your feet flat on the floor with your thighs parallel to the ground and your spine straight). Inhale slowly and deeply, then hold your breath while performing ten anal contractions. Take a small sniff of air through your nose, then exhale slowly out the mouth. Repeat ten times. You can increase the number of contractions per breath and the number of repetitions once you are comfortable with this exercise.

EMOTIONAL SUPPORT

We feel that it is important to say a few words about emotional support systems and coping mechanisms. The training you are about to begin is very rigorous, especially on an emotional level. You will be working with emotions and issues that most people only deal with on the therapist's couch, or in support groups. You may not have the formal support network that goes along with these more traditional paths. It is important that you develop a network of your own before you become embroiled in the more intense stages of energy work. Make a list of the sources of emotional support available to you. These may or may not include your partner (if you are practicing with a partner), your friends and family, your journal, fellow practitioners, or a professional counselor.

YOUR PARTNER

You and your partner should already be committed to helping each other through the emotional and spiritual crises that may arise, and you should each feel that you can rely on the other to do this. However, there are two considerations when going to your partner for help. First, remember that your partner is not a detached observer with an outside perspective. He or she is intimately involved in the process you are going through and may not be able to see patterns that you will need to identify. Second, remember that your partner may be experiencing his or her own emotional traumas at the same time, and may not be able to offer the degree of support that you need. Neither of these things is the fault of your partner—we are all human—but you must realize that there will be problems that your partner may not be able to help you solve.

YOUR FAMILY AND FRIENDS

While your family and friends may be an excellent source of emotional support, you should be very careful who you talk to about your sexual practice. Our society's taboos make it difficult for others to talk about sex on a normal level, and most people will not be familiar enough with the concept of sacred sex to really understand what you are trying to do. Make sure that the people you talk to about your practice are open-minded enough to honestly listen to what you are saying.

YOUR JOURNAL

We recommend keeping a journal of your practice for two reasons:

- You will have a record that you can refer to as you go, and that can help you gain perspective on your progress.
- You will have a place where you can say anything you need to say without worrying that someone is judging you for it.

FELLOW PRACTITIONERS

It may be difficult to find people who are doing the same kinds of things you are doing, but it's worth it. People who are learning the same kinds of lessons you are trying to learn will understand exactly what you are going through and will be able to offer advice and comfort.

PROFESSIONAL COUNSELING: WHEN DO YOU NEED IT?

If you are experiencing depression severe enough to keep you from functioning normally—if you are having problems getting out of bed, going to work, socializing with friends, or just generally participating in life—you should consider professional counseling. Many people who attempt to deliberately modify their normal energy patterns often experience periods where they want to retreat into seclusion. This is normal, but if you find yourself unwilling or unable to face the reality of day-to-day living, or if you are severely depressed or suicidal, you should get help at once. It is easy to get in over your head without realizing it, and there is always a possibility that you won't be able to get out again without help. Sometimes a friend or fellow practitioner may be able to help, but if this doesn't work, it is very important that you seek professional counseling. It may also be a good idea for you to decrease your practice until you have reached a more stable mindset, and then continue your practice at a slower pace.

When choosing a counselor, be cautious. Be wary of those who want to prescribe mood-altering medication, especially as a long-term solution. While there are people whose problems are the result of chemical imbalances, there are many others taking medication—and experiencing the resulting negative side effects—when their problems could be dealt with in other ways. Ideally, your counselor should be someone you can trust and who you can talk comfortably with. If you try a counselor and don't seem to be making any progress after a few months, you should look for another one.

ENDNOTES

1. *Food for Thought: A New Look at Food and Behavior,* by Saul and Jo Anne Miller, offers an excellent discussion on the relationship between food and consciousness. The Millers use the terms "expansive" and "contractive" to describe the action of food on consciousness. Contractive foods are foods that increase the earth-tide within the body; expansive foods are those that increase the star-tide.

2. Dr. Jean Shinoda Bolen's books, *Goddesses in Every Woman* and *Gods in Every Man* are excellent starting points for finding links between your personas and mythological figures.

SEVEN

Creating Polarity: Solo Exercises

The key to altering consciousness is to become aware of it. As you learn to be aware of your state of consciousness, it will become easier for you to change. This will allow you to "tune in" desired states of consciousness that are appropriate to your goals.

RELEASING TENSION

Being tense is a state of consciousness, and like all states of consciousness is reflected in the body as well as the mind. It is important to learn how to notice tension as it begins to build, and how to dissipate it. Tension can interfere with your ability to think and function, and make you physically as well as psychically ill.

One of the simplest ways to release tension is to bring yourself to orgasm. In many of the exercises described below, orgasm will be a part of the process. If you still feel the need to relax, you can try other things.

To release tension, try kneeling or sitting on the ground, placing your palms flat on the ground. Breathe deeply and slowly, and visualize tension flowing easily out of your body, down your arms, and into the ground. Don't try to push the tension out, but just let it find its way back to the earth. When you feel relaxed, stop.

A second method of releasing tension is to lie down in a comfortable position, and to deliberately tense and then release every muscle in your body. You may have to tense and release several times before you feel sufficiently relaxed.

Each person relaxes in different ways, and you may have your own methods. If you are feeling very mental, a physical activity is called for, like going for a walk, washing dishes or perhaps getting a massage. If you are feeling very physical, a mental activity is required, like daydreaming or listening to light music. If you cannot tell what kind of stress you are experiencing, try a mental activity first, and if this doesn't work, you can always try being physical next.

Being able to release tension is important for practicing the various techniques in this book, because they can cause tensions to surface. It is important to know how to dissipate them before they interfere with your well-being.

BREATHING

There are four basic modes of breathing you will need to know. These can be combined with each other to achieve a variety of effects.

Deep slow breathing activates the parasympathetic nervous system, enhances rational thought, and promotes calmness and clarity. This type of breathing enhances celestial consciousness, and can be used by men to delay ejaculation and by women to delay orgasm.

Fast, hard breathing activates the sympathetic nervous system, stimulates adrenaline production, intensifies emotions, makes rational thought difficult, and enhances the body's ability to perform strenuous physical activity. This kind of breathing enhances terrestrial consciousness, and can be used to increase your level of arousal.

Synchronous breathing increases intimacy and attunes you to your partner. To perform synchronous breathing, you and your partner match each other: you inhale as he inhales, and you exhale as he exhales. This type of breathing tends to decrease arousal, but increases attunement and creates a sense of peace between two people. (Note: if you can do this type of breathing for a few minutes, you can start to take on the same mood that your partner is in. If one of you is in a bad mood, that person should match the breathing of the one who is not in a bad mood.)

Complementary breathing strengthens polarity and, in sexual situations, increases arousal. To perform complementary breathing, you and your partner breathe in reverse: one inhales as the other exhales, and vice versa.

BREATHING FOR BEGINNERS

If you have never practiced a discipline that involved specific breathing techniques, you might want to try simply sitting down for a few minutes in a comfortable position and breathing deeply and slowly. If you can only take a few long breaths before feeling lightheaded, you may want to alternate a long breath with a few normal breaths.

If you are interested in trying a more traditional breathing technique, try this. Sit in a comfortable position. Inhale slowly and deeply through the nose, until your lungs are completely full, to a count of ten. Hold your breath, with the feeling of pressing the air down into your stomach, for a count of five, then take a quick sniff of air, and exhale very slowly through your mouth, to a count of fifteen or more. Hold the breath again, for a count of five. The quick sniff of air will help you release the pent-up air slowly and with control, rather than in an explosive rush. As you master this technique, you can increase the count for each step of the breathing cycle; just make sure that the exhale is always longer than the inhale.

Try out all four types of breathing, and notice how your awareness changes as you switch, or as you practice them with a partner.

MEDITATION

Some people confuse meditation with breathing exercises and elaborate visualizations, but these techniques are not meditation (although they can make meditation easier, especially at the beginning levels). Meditation is, very simply, the art of paying attention. Meditation should not be an escape from reality, but a way of changing your attitude about reality by changing your focus, and deliberately choosing the parts of reality that you pay attention to. When you meditate, you begin to develop your awareness of your environment, of your physical condition, of your state of mind, and of divine consciousness.

You can spend a lot of time perfecting breathing techniques, and these techniques will give you greater control over your energetic condition, but all you have to do to meditate is pay attention. Naturally, the fewer distractions you must deal with, the easier it will be for you to pay attention to the more subtle things. This is why meditation is usually taught in a quiet, peaceful environment where the only distraction you will encounter is yourself. However, the goal of meditation is not to permanently retreat into this quiet, peaceful environment. The goal is to learn to maintain this state of careful awareness in your everyday life, in spite of the many distractions you must deal with. Many people make the mistake of assuming that meditation is only something you can do at a retreat, or in a special class, or when you are alone. In fact, meditation can be done any time and at any place, and any activity can become a meditation.

To turn any activity into a meditation, simply practice it with awareness. Pretend that you have never performed this activity before, and observe yourself doing it as if you are doing it for the first time. If you are sweeping the floor, pay close attention to the way the bristles run over the floor, the way your body moves in order to push the broom, the things you think as you are pushing the broom. Be aware of the sounds around you, the way the air moves as you move through it, the way your energy moves as you sweep. It sounds simple—and it is—but it is not easy. We are conditioned to live in the future and in the past. While our bodies go through the motions of life, our minds are often in the future: planning the next activity, thinking about things that must be done, anticipating future events; or in the past: reliving yesterday's conversation, trying to remember whether or not something got done, worrying about the consequences of yesterday's actions. The happiness that comes from living in the moment is a result of simply being aware of your present existence. How can you enjoy what you don't notice?

The application for meditation in sex is obvious—when do you enjoy sex most? When you are thinking about unpaid bills, the dirty laundry, the thing that your co-worker said to you the other day? Or when you are paying attention to the sensation of your partner's skin on yours, the sound of your partner's breathing, the way your partner's hair tickles your neck? Sacred sex begins with meditative sex. In order to understand the flow of energies between you and your partner, you must first be aware of it.

VISUALIZATION

Visualizing the flow of energy and breath in the body is a powerful tool in energy work. However, you should not assume that the visualization is an accurate picture of what is actually occurring in your body. The image of energy flowing through your body is not the energy itself—it is merely an interface through which that energy can be encouraged to move. It is a way of "getting a handle" on it, so that you can mentally direct it.

As a culture, we rely very heavily on visual stimuli, and many of our non-visual activities are phrased in visual terms. For example, when we understand how another person is feeling, we say that we can "see" their point. When we are trying to calculate the consequences of a possible action, we are "looking before we leap." While many people are visually oriented, there are also people who prefer to rely on aural stimuli (I "hear" what you're saying) or kinesthetic stimuli (I really "feel" for you).

If you have difficulty using visualization, it is fine to modify any of the exercises in this book. If you tend to experience energy as sound, focus on that. If you can feel the energy as a sensation of heat or as a vibration moving through your body, then use those feelings to control your energy flow. You may even experience energetic changes as emotional shifts.

Many people in the New Age movement have lost sight of the fact that visualization is a tool, not an end in itself. It's an instrument for people who do not have the ability to consciously alter their patterns of energy flow—an interface between the mind and the energetic body. The goal of visualization is not to create a perfect image, but to reach a point where you can control your energetic body without needing to rely on an exercise. The visualization is a way to ask your body to conform to an energetic state so that you can feel what that state is like, and then learn to return to it. When you have attained a level of awareness where you do not need to use an image to manipulate your energy flow, the visualization can be dispensed with altogether.

COLOR VISUALIZATION

You can use breathing in conjunction with color visualizations to alter the energetic condition of your body. Different colors produce different effects. Because colors also have personal meaning, and because these personal meanings may depend on your mood at the time that you perform this exercise, it is best to try a wide range of colors until you find the ones that work best for you. The colors are used as symbols for mental and emotional states in order to infuse yourself with that state. If you symbolize the states differently (as imagined sounds or physical sensations, for example), you can substitute these for colors.

Sit or lie comfortably with your eyes closed. Begin to breathe. As you inhale, imagine colored light (of the color you've chosen) entering your body with the air, and filling up your body. As you exhale, imagine that you are breathing out a muddy brown. As you blow the brown away from you, it becomes clear and mingles with the air around you. Continue to do this until your body is filled with the color you have chosen to inhale.

You can also try a variation on this exercise. Instead of breathing the color in through the nose and/or mouth, try breathing it in through all the pores of your body. The muddy brown can be either exhaled through the nose and/or mouth, or, if it is more comfortable, out through the pores. This exercise can be used for cleansing or for altering your mood. It can also be used magically. Before a working, breathe in a color appropriate to the spell or ritual action you wish to perform.

COMPLEX VISUALIZATION

Instead of simple colors, it is possible to use complex images in the previous exercise. You can fill your body with the image and scent of a single, perfect, dew-covered rose. You can fill your body with the image of the Full Moon on a winter's night. This can be done as a way of cleansing the body, as above, or can be done after cleansing. Choose images that are both appropriate to the mood you are trying to invoke and that are personally symbolic.

VISUALIZATIONS FOR THE ENERGY CENTERS

While you can visualize your whole body being filled by a color or an image, it is also possible to concentrate on a single energy center (or simply a single portion of the body) when doing the above exercises. You could imagine a blue star filling your third eye center, or you could imagine spheres of mother of pearl at each fingertip. Follow your instincts: What feels good? What feels appropriate? Again, this can be done as a cleansing visualization or after you have been cleansed.

DEITY VISUALIZATIONS

Popular psychologists are currently exploring the idea that men and women can use mythology as a way of understanding themselves.

Women are typically encouraged to "find the goddesses within" and men, likewise, to "find the gods within." This is good as far as it goes, but it should be realized that men may tune in to goddesses and women may tune in to gods. In fact, in the ancient world it was just as common for goddesses to be served by priests as by priestesses, and for gods to be served by priestesses as by priests. Each gender's way of approaching a particular deity is valid and should be respected. The assumption that only women tune into the goddess and men tune into the god is a very sexist belief, and has the effect of distancing men from their connection with the Divine Feminine and of distancing women from their connection with the Divine Masculine.

If you recognize a certain deity as expressing itself through you, you may wish to try invoking it more fully. This is similar to doing complex visualizations, except that you bring into your body symbols associated with a deity (or archetype), or an image of the deity (or archetype) itself. Your breathing should reflect the type of deity you are invoking. For instance, if you are visualizing Pan, breathe fast and hard to increase awareness of terrestrial consciousness. Imagine horns rising from your head. Grin mischievously. Notice the physical sensations that arise. Let your body begin to follow the pattern that you are bringing into it.

This can be a very intense exercise. As always, if it feels uncomfortable, try to do it just a little bit longer, and if the discomfort remains, stop.

MASTURBATION

Masturbation is crucial to your practice of transformative sex for a number of reasons. Masturbation enhances your control of your physical and energetic bodies. It allows you to learn in great detail how your body works sexually and energetically. For those who experience sexual dysfunction, self-stimulation can be a method of self-treatment.

Masturbation allows you to practice directing the flow of sexual energy in your body without the distraction of a partner whose needs must be met. It also frees you from the need to coordinate schedules and desires with your partner in order to master the basic exercises necessary for you to participate in the Sexual Mysteries. Self-stimulation also enhances sexual health, as sexual arousal and orgasm cause beneficial hormones to be released into the bloodstream, which in turn can improve your mood and alleviate the physiological and emotional effects of stress.

Masturbation can be used between sexual encounters to bleed off a certain amount of the sexual tension that prevents you from fully merging energetically with your partner. It allows you to focus on the exchange of energy with your partner rather than focusing on achieving orgasm.

FANTASY AND MASTURBATION

Many people are inhibited in their fantasy lives as well as their real lives. Can you fantasize about other people besides your partner, or is that being unfaithful? Is it okay for a person to fantasize about rape, or does this mean he or she is sick? Can you fantasize about having sex with a porpoise, or is that perverted? Another concern is that by fantasizing about something, you "put energy" into having it manifest. Some fantasies would be terrible if they really happened.

Your mind is the only thing you truly own, so have fun with it. You are officially given permission to fantasize about having sex with animals, monsters, strangers, household appliances, inanimate objects, and so on. In fact, try imagining something outrageous while masturbating, and see if you can "get into it" enough to orgasm. Why not? As for worrying about making fantasies manifest, don't. The point of having a fantasy is sometimes just to have the fantasy. Before fantasizing, decide whether your fantasy is something you really want to happen. If you don't want it to happen in real life, it won't. The important thing is to recognize the very crucial barrier between imagination and reality. Fantasies are harmless, as long as you don't allow them to change the way you deal with real people.

Fantasy should be a way to explore alternate realities. A repressed fantasy can become a fixation, but a healthy fantasy life is as rich and varied as a real life—even more so, because there are no limits to your imagination.

MASTURBATION AS MEDITATION: ENERGETIC EXERCISES

Each of the exercises described below can be done with a partner, but they should be practiced alone first, so that you will be free to focus on the movement of energy through your body.

PROLONGING AROUSAL

One of the simplest exercises you can do is to practice prolonging arousal. This exercise is usually prescribed by sex therapists for men who suffer from premature ejaculation, and is an effective treatment for this condition. Its benefits, however, are by no means limited to men. Some people will experience a light trance state during this exercise. Most will find that they feel more sensual after doing this regularly for a week or two. You are conditioning your body to handle the energies that build during a prolonged plateau phase. If you practice any magical discipline, you will find that your ability to build and maintain a charge during ritual work will improve as a result of performing this exercise regularly.

Stimulate yourself until you reach the moment before orgasm ("the point of no return," the last possible moment at which you can refrain from orgasming). At this point, stop and breathe slowly and deeply until the desire to orgasm recedes. Do this several times, each time reaching the edge of orgasm and pulling back. An advanced form of this exercise is done by simply slowing down and reducing self-stimulation, rather than stopping completely.

THE SQUEEZE TECHNIQUE

It is possible for men to stop orgasm from occurring by firmly squeezing the penis between thumb and finger. If a man feels he is getting close to orgasm too quickly, he can place his thumb on the underside of the shaft, just beneath the head of the penis, and his first two fingers on top, again just below the head. Squeeze firmly and hold. The desire to orgasm should diminish, and it is likely that the penis will become slightly deflated. If orgasm has already begun, let go and allow the ejaculation to occur. Never attempt to stop ejaculation once it has begun.

Empathic Sex Visualization

While masturbating and fantasizing about a lover, imagine that you are the person you are masturbating about. Imagine how you feel to that other person. Then, take this a step further and try to imagine the sensations of both you and your lover simultaneously. Imagine you are both people at once. This exercise may seem simple in its effects, but will have profound influences on how you experience orgasms and on how you relate to your sexual partner or partners.

The Succubus/Incubus Visualization

Certain spirit entities interact with people through sexual imagery. "Succubus" is the name given to a female spirit of this type, while "incubus" is the male name. Succubi and incubi are, not surprisingly, considered "evil spirits" by sexually repressive religions. The terms "good" and "evil" are irrelevant to the Sexual Mysteries. Each person must judge for themselves whether another being's influences are beneficial or harmful, and we should remember that what is appropriate for one person may be inappropriate for another.

It is possible to interact with spirit guides through sexual fantasy. While masturbating, imagine you are having sex with a stranger. The appearance can be anything you wish, but should not resemble any person you know. Imagine asking this lover for wisdom or guidance in some aspect of your life, then stimulate yourself as usual. When you are near orgasm, imagine that your lover presses his or her mouth near your

ear and whispers something as you climax. Because you are climaxing, you are distracted and do not consciously hear what is said. However, you know that something has been communicated to you at a deeper level of your mind. The wisdom or guidance you have asked for has been given to you, and will begin to express itself in your life. In some cases, it may surface almost immediately and you will consciously know what you have been told. This exercise is an excellent way to establish a contact with an otherworld guide.

CHARGING THE ENERGY CENTERS

This exercise teaches you to transmute sexual energy by pulling it up the spine from the root center to each of the other centers. Once you have mastered this exercise, you can use it to correct imbalance in the centers or to heal minor physical illnesses. Furthermore, it is not even essential that you bring the energy up to one of the main energy centers. As we have stated before, the centers on the spine are major points of flux, but the entire body is an energy conduit, and energy can be directed toward any portion of the body.

Stimulate yourself, focusing your attention on your pelvic area and on your root center. Feel the energy building up in the root center. Once you have built up a significant amount of energy, pull it up to your navel center, and allow it to build there. Imagine the energy traveling up from your root center to your navel center, and then back down again to form a complete circuit. When you have stabilized this flow, pull the energy up to the solar plexus. Continue until the energy is flowing all the way from your root to your crown, and then back down again. When you are finished, allow the energy to fall back down to the root center, and release the excess through orgasm.

This exercise can also be done in reverse order, bringing energy down from the crown to the root.

Another exercise you can try is this: Build up to an orgasm, then instead of climaxing, direct the orgasmic tension upwards and inwards (if you are a male) or downwards and outwards (if you are a female). If this is done correctly, you will have a distinctly different experience than when you normally orgasm. It will likely not feel as intense or exciting as a regular orgasm, but try exploring it anyway. This exercise allows you to gain a fundamental understanding of how members of the opposite sex experience orgasm. To intensify this experience, women can imagine that their clitoris is a penis, shooting semen, and men can imagine that they are receiving a penis in an imaginary vagina.

Breathing and Orgasm

As you approach orgasm, experiment with different sorts of breathing. What happens when you breathe fast and hard? Slow and deep? What happens when you moan? What effect do different sounds have? Try and see.

ORGASM AND ENERGY CENTERS

Until now, the masturbation exercises we have presented have been concerned with the control of energy during a state of arousal. The next exercise focuses on the control of energy which would otherwise be released during orgasm, and as a result, is much more difficult.

Stimulate yourself until you reach the moment before orgasm (slowing down as you get closer to orgasm helps), then stop and pull the accumulated energy in your root center up to your heart center while breathing deeply and slowly. Allow this energy to permeate your heart center. After a minute or two, resume self-stimulation. Repeat this process two to five more times, then allow yourself to orgasm.

Don't be discouraged if you are unable to finish this exercise before orgasming. Just keep practicing.

This exercise can be done with any energy center. We recommend beginning with the heart center because consistent practice of this exercise can alleviate loneliness, depression, jealousy, anxiety, and other types of insecurity that plague many people. Once you've begun dealing with these emotions, you will find yourself much more able to face the rest of your life.

EXPANDING YOUR ENERGY FLOW

While the energy centers are a good place to start your energy work, you ultimately want to be able to control the flow of energy through every part of your body. This next exercise teaches you to flood your entire body with the energy of orgasm. Rather than experiencing an orgasm focused exclusively in the root center, you feel the orgasm throughout your whole body.

Stimulate yourself until you reach the moment before orgasm. At this point, stop, breathe deeply and slowly, and imagine the energy expanding outward from your root center in a sphere, to encompass your entire body. As this happens, you may feel a floating sensation, or feel as if your body is being engulfed in a series of waves. Do not resist the sensation. Let yourself be rocked until you return to normal consciousness. (If you do not experience these sensations immediately, don't worry. This one can take months to get, depending on your current level of skill and how frequently you practice.)

You should take this one slowly, especially at first. You may find that you feel "spacy" or "out of it" after performing this exercise. If so, be sure to use the exercise for increasing the earth-tide, or to ground in your own way.

Continuous Orgasm

This exercise induces a floating or pulsating sensation very similar to the one described in the previous exercise, but more intense. The continuous orgasm meditation requires very precise control of your body. You must remain just on the edge of orgasm for an extended period of time. Sound like a lot of work? It is—but it can also induce an altered state of consciousness that is both ecstatic and transcendent.

Stimulate yourself slowly but steadily, breathing deeply, until you have reached the moment just before orgasm. Stop and slow your breathing down until the urge to orgasm has receded slightly, then masturbate very gently until you are right back on the edge again. Stop and slow your breathing down until the urge recedes again, and repeat. Eventually, you will reach a level of skill where you know instinctively exactly how long to pause and how much stimulation it takes to bring you right back to the edge. The shorter you can make the space between stopping and starting, the better.

Now for the crucial second part of this exercise. As you do the above, begin contracting the PC muscle as described in Chapter Six, and imagine these contractions pumping energy upwards throughout your body. At first, these contractions may seem to be a distraction, and coordinating them with self-stimulation may be very frustrating. Practice, practice, practice.

SEPARATING EJACULATION FROM ORGASM

Many Tantric practices are designed to teach men to separate ejaculation from orgasm. While this is a very useful technique, which allows for extended sexual encounters and multiple orgasm for the male, it must be understood that loss of ejaculate does not necessarily mean a loss of vitality. Don't allow yourself to fall into the trap of being selfish with your energy out of fear. Instead, focus on learning to build power by sharing energy with your partner, and on learning to bring energy into your own body whenever you need it.

Orgasming without ejaculation is a veritable mystery. In order to experience it, one must simply try it. Keep in mind that it is a matter of approaching orgasm, then changing the form of sexual stimulation and simultaneously of mentally directing the energy of the orgasm upwards into the body. For instance, a man who is masturbating could come very close to climax, then change the way he is using his hand to stimulate himself at the same time as he imagines the orgasm shooting up inside himself. This is discussed further in Chapter Nine.

SEXUAL ETHICS

While many religions consider most sex to be immoral, the Sexual Mysteries focus instead on the moral use of sex. The following standards should always apply.

- It is never acceptable to use sacred sexuality as an excuse to have sex with another person against their will, or to have an affair that violates a commitment you have made with a partner.

- It is never acceptable to pressure another person into having sex with you.

- It is never acceptable to use what you have learned from the Sexual Mysteries to manipulate other people's energy against their will or to take energy from them without their consent.

CONSIDERATIONS IN PARTNER WORK

There are a number of important considerations in practicing transformational sex with a partner. It is absolutely imperative that the person you choose be someone you can trust completely. Trust is more important than physical attractiveness, more important than social standing, more important than anything. The person you choose to be your partner is going to see parts of your psyche that you don't even know exist. Your partner is going to see you at your lowest, while you are feeling depressed, enraged, violated, ecstatic, despairing, and idiotic. You are going to say things to this person that you will regret later. You will admit things to this person that you have never told anyone. By agreeing to undertake these practices, you place yourself in a position of extreme vulnerability, and it is crucial that you choose a partner who is worthy of this responsibility. At the same time, you need to be certain that you are able to offer this same kind of commitment to your partner, because

you're going to be getting your hands dirty together. An unwillingness to make a very deep commitment to each other before beginning these practices can have devastating results for both of you.

Should you practice Tantra with your current partner? They may or may not be interested. If they aren't, you may need to confine your exploration of sacred sexuality to solo practice. Even if you think your current partner would be open to the idea, you should be very careful in the way that you present it to them. Many people, when told that their partner wants to start changing their sex lives, will start to feel insecure about the state of their relationship. They may wonder: "Do you want to study sacred sex because I'm no good in bed? Are you unhappy with me? Don't we already have a spiritual connection?" It will be up to you to present your desire to practice these exercises with your partner in a non-threatening way, and to reassure them that your goal is to expand your current relationship and to include them in your spiritual explorations, rather than to patch up existing inadequacies.

Do you want your sex life with your partner to consist solely of spiritual exercise? Do you want your lovemaking with your partner to be directly linked to your spiritual goals? This puts a lot of pressure on both you and your partner, and can lead to the disintegration of your relationship if both people are not very committed, both to the Sexual Mysteries and to the relationship. The purpose of transformational sex is the sharing of energy in order to further each other's spiritual growth. The kinds of games that lovers often play may add spice to the relationship, but they can also interfere with your spiritual development. Many people who mix romantic love with sacred sex find that their spiritual goals become confused with the goals of the love relationship, and they begin to measure their spiritual growth by the stability of the love relationship, and vice versa.

What if your partner is not interested in practicing this mode of spirituality with you? Our society's monogamous morality frowns upon multiple sexual partners, and even if you are not married, it is usually very difficult to have both a sacred lover and a romantic lover without at least one partner (if not both) becoming jealous. In addition, maintaining a second relationship behind your primary partner's back is extremely foolish, as it will very likely blow up in your face one day. In addition, it can create guilt that will eventually interfere with the very spiritual growth that you are trying to achieve. If your partner is uninterested in or unwilling to practice with you, you are much better off practicing on your own, and applying the knowledge you gain to your relationship and other areas of your life.

EIGHT

Completing the Circuit:
Partner Exercises

T he exercises in this chapter are specifically designed to help you
to integrate your energies harmoniously with a partner. This
integration creates balance both within the self and between
partners, which is the goal of sacred sex.

Once you have tried an exercise, feel free to experiment with various elements. As your intuition develops, learn to follow it. Try out different positions and different types of breathing. Combine them with other exercises from this book and from other sources. Play, experiment and grow.

Before you begin any of these exercises, you may perform any meditation or activity that clears your mind and calms you down, such as taking a shower, walking, exercising, meditation or deep breathing. Prepare your space as appropriate, and make sure that lubricants, birth control, massage oil and anything else you will need are close at hand. Adjust the lighting. Candlelight is very appropriate for sacred sex. Burn incense and play music if desired. By preparing everything ahead of time, you and your partner will be freed from distractions, allowing the two of you to focus more completely on each other. Spontaneity is a part of this practice, and you may find that many energy work sessions become lovemaking sessions. This is not a sign of weakness or lack of discipline. It is a sign that you are integrating your spirituality into your sexuality, which will increase your intimacy as a couple.

It is a good idea to try each of these exercises for at least a few minutes to give yourself enough time to explore the technique, but do not feel obligated to perform them any longer than you feel you need to. Some of these techniques may produce some discomfort, or strange sensations that might make you uneasy. It is up to you to decide whether these feelings indicate a problem or are simply unfamiliar. Stop when you want. Come back to them when you want. Disciplined practice is important, but forcing yourself beyond your limits is both unnecessary and dangerous. It is better to err on the side of caution than to make yourself ill.

We recommend trying these exercises using both synchronous and complementary breathing, inhaling and exhaling both slowly and quickly. Once you have tried these combinations, pick the ones that seem to have the best effect for you. Many of these exercises also work without any special breathing techniques, but the effect achieved will not be as dramatic and may be harder to control.

After performing any of the exercises described in this book, notice if you feel too grounded or too ungrounded. If you do feel uncomfortable, be sure to take care of this by doing the exercises for strengthening the star-tide (to become less grounded) or the earth-tide (to become more grounded) described in Chapter Four.

THE ENERGETICS OF SEX

As you start experiencing transformational sex, you and your partner will begin to experience role reversals. Each of you will start taking on the other person's attitudes, emotional patterns, and sometimes even physical problems. Parallel experiences may occur: for instance, one of you may have and resolve some specific difficulty, and a few months later your partner will face the same issues. As partners, you serve as mirrors for each other. There are several advantages to this. Often, you will find that the two of you are complementary—that your partner will be able to transmute energy that cannot, and vice versa. Learn from each other's strengths, and don't be afraid to ask each other for help.

THE SECRET OF TRANSFORMATIONAL SEX

The secret to this type of mystical sex is to keep the energy flowing through the circuit, even without physical motion. The man must keep thrusting with his mind, even though he has stopped thrusting with his body. The woman must continue to receive energy from the man with her mind, even though she has also stopped moving. At the intermediate stage, you can use PC contractions to "pump" the energy through your body in the desired direction, but at the advanced stage, the energy is moved solely through mental direction.

Normal sex occurs in four stages: arousal, plateau, orgasm, and afterglow. It involves a physical and energetic release. In normal sex, both partners are often focused on orgasm as the main goal of intercourse. Transformational sex, on the other hand, involves the transmutation of at least part of the energy which would be released in orgasm. Its main goal is transformation of the self through the transmutation of sexual energy, and sexual release may or may not occur. During transformational sex, you experience arousal, but when you reach the plateau stage, you remain there for a much longer time, directing the energy to a specific purpose.

The main characteristic of transformational sex is the conscious sharing of energy, which increases the flow of energy through both partners. As with other spiritual practices, this type of sex breaks through resistances that have been built as a protection against internal or external pressures. You will be forced to face emotional problems that you have been avoiding for years, and to re-examine mental conditioning that has buffered you from the vicissitudes of life. When you remove this conditioning, you will be vulnerable again while you attempt to find new ways of interacting with people and resolving situations.

In addition, you will be forced to look at the parts of yourself that you least want to see. Changing bad habits is never fun. It's going to hurt, and the more you resist these changes, the more painful they are going to be. Surrendering to the powerful forces that transformational sex arouse is difficult, but it's also the best way to avoid a great deal of change-generated stress.

Transformational sex is powerful because it is not static. Transformation requires movement. By sharing energy with your partner, you increase the movement of energy in your own body, breaking through resistances and energetic blockages. Furthermore, you and your partner will have different areas of competence. Your partner will be able to handle types of energy flow that you will not, and vice versa. This means that the potential rate of change is greater than you could achieve on your own, but it also means that you each assume the responsibility of helping the other with emotional or energetic problems.

We cannot emphasize enough the importance of shared energy. Sharing energy with your partner is the defining characteristic of transformational sex. Traditional Eastern Tantra, with its focus on energy conservation, can distract you from this goal. Many practitioners misunderstand the goal of Tantric sex, and find themselves hoarding energy. They try to steal energy from their partner and keep it for themselves, rather than giving completely of themselves and receiving the same from their partners. Taken to an extreme, this philosophy of conservation can develop into a neurotic paranoia. It encourages a type of energy vampirism in which the more skilled practitioner uses their partner to build a store of energy via sex and then takes all the energy raised for themselves, draining their partner.

ORAL SEX

Oral sex differs from vaginal sex energetically, as it is not procreative, and it is often much more intense than vaginal penetration. For the woman, oral sex means a more direct type of stimulation—clitoral rather than vaginal. Vaginal orgasms usually involve a pulling of energy up from the root center, and so enhance the celestial polarity. Clitoral orgasms, on the other hand, direct the woman's energy downwards (crown to root), strengthening the terrestrial polarity, and are therefore very similar to male orgasms. (As a side note, women may try stimulating the clitoris while engaging in vaginal sex or using a vibrator; men can try penile stimulation combined with anal penetration. It is thus possible to experience both types of orgasms at once.)

During oral sex, the person who is doing the stimulating can take energy in through the mouth or third eye center and bring it down to their root center. If you are engaged in mutual oral sex, the other person can then "drink" that same energy and bring it down their spine to their root center and give it back to the first person. This stimulates creativity and psychic sensitivity, and is also an ideal method for achieving a trance state, especially when stimulation is slow and steady.

Obviously, genital hygiene is important. If you or your partner have any qualms about oral sex, don't hesitate to wash your genitals with water (and a mild soap, if you feel the need). However, as long as neither of you is infected with a sexually transmitted disease, there is no reason to avoid ingestion of the sexual fluids. They are "clean" and, in fact, contain pheromones and other compounds that can increase sexual excitement.

If sexually transmitted disease is a consideration, you can purchase unlubricated condoms and dental dams. Dental dams are thin pieces of latex which are placed over the woman's pubic area before oral sex to prevent the ingestion of vaginal secretions. Neither condoms nor dental dams will affect the transfer of energy. The fluids can be charged with energy, but they are not necessary for this transfer of energy to take place. Condoms and dental dams do taste like latex, which some find unpleasant.

If your partner objects to the taste of your sexual fluids, but would like to try to acquire the taste, there is a way to adjust slowly. Before you have sex, but after you are aroused, take a little bit of your own sexual fluid and rub it onto your lips, then kiss your partner. Eventually, he or she will begin to associate the taste of your fluids with sexual excitement, and will no longer be bothered by the taste of oral sex. If your partner is unwilling to try this, you can try purchasing one of the numerous flavored lotions which are designed specifically for the purpose of making oral sex more palatable. If you use a flavored lotion, be sure to urinate and wash your genitals shortly after sex to reduce the risk of urinary tract and (in women, vaginal) infections.

Depending on how your bodies fit together, you may want to vary the position in which you perform oral sex, especially if you intend to both give and receive at the same time. For reciprocal oral sex, how comfortable a particular position is depends on the difference in size between you and your partner. If you and your partner are roughly the same size, the woman-on-top or woman-on-bottom positions work well. If there is a significant size difference, you may be more comfortable lying on your sides, facing each other.

While reciprocal oral sex can be exciting, it can also be a little bit distracting. You may get so swept up in the sensations that you are unable to concentrate on what you are doing. If only one person is receiving stimulation, you will both have an easier time paying attention to the energy flow, and the person who is doing the stimulating can focus on what they are doing. Just be sure that the position you choose allows both you and your partner to be relaxed and comfortable.

As an exercise, while your partner stimulates you orally, notice what this stimulation does to your energy flow. Imagine energy flowing into your crown, and traveling down through your root center. The person giving should drink this energy in, and pull it down their spine, allowing it to flow out their root center and back to the universe.

Receiving oral sex in an upside-down position is one way to reverse the flow of energy which normally occurs during oral sex. In addition, it is relatively easy to attain trance states in upside-down positions. However, upside-down positions often require a fair amount of strength and the ability to maintain your balance even during orgasm. Furthermore, these positions can place large amounts of pressure on the neck and shoulders (depending on the position). They can be dangerous unless your partner is strong enough (and quick enough!) to catch you if you start to lose control and fall. The easiest (and safest) way to achieve this sensation is to hang your head over the edge of the bed while your partner stimulates you.

ANAL SEX

In spite of increasing sexual awareness in America, the taboo against anal sex is still quite strong. Because of this, if you are able to break this taboo, you will release a tremendous amount of emotional and psychic energy. Many traditional Tantric writings warn against anal sex as dangerous, but most of these prohibitions arise from cultural taboos.

Anal stimulation can have tremendous emotional repercussions, especially the first few times. You may experience intense sadness, anger, humiliation, or depression, all of which will seem to be unconnected to what is actually happening. This occurs because of a phenomenon that Wilhelm Reich called "armoring." When you experience traumatic experiences, you store the resultant emotions as muscular tension in various areas of your body. When this tension is released, the emotions associated with that tension are also released. If you have never experimented with anality before, it is a good idea to start with anal massage (described in Chapter Four), and perhaps to experiment with a small flexible dildo or vibrator.

Be sure that you go slowly and carefully, especially if you are new to anal sex. Don't overdo it. The same precautions that applied to anal massage (cleanliness and caution) also apply to anal sex. After anal sex, be sure to wash your fingers and anything else that may have been inserted into your partner's anus. Never insert anything into the vagina that has been inserted into the anus without washing it first! A serious infection could occur otherwise.

For the man who is particularly daring, anal sex is an excellent way to experience your partner's role during sex. The woman can penetrate the man anally with either a vibrator or a dildo, held in her hand or fastened with a harness. The woman should focus on bringing her energy down from the crown to the root center, and on thrusting that energy into the man. The man should focus on receiving the energy from his partner and bringing it up through his root center to his crown center, then returning it to the universe.

A note for beginners: Erotic movies often depict anal sex in which the recipient is kneeling on hands and knees, "doggy-style." For experienced practitioners this position may be desirable, as it allows for deep penetration, but beginners may want to try something a little less intense. The recipient should lie flat on his or her stomach, with a small pillow under the hips.

ATTUNING TO YOUR PARTNER

One of the best ways to begin a session with your partner is to synchronize your body's energy with theirs. There are a number of ways to do this. After working with your partner for a while, you will discover the one that works best for you.

One of the simplest ways is to lie down together (unclothed, if possible), either facing each other, or with one person behind the other. Start by listening to each other's breathing, then try to match it. As your partner inhales, do the same, and as he or she exhales, follow. Continue until you feel ready to begin another exercise.

MASSAGE AND BODY WORK

Another nice way to start is to give your partner a massage (even a quick one), or to have your partner lie down while you stroke them with your hands, a piece of fur, a silk cloth, a feather, etc. Or have your partner lie still while you cover him or her with slow, firm kisses. These sorts of things increase intimacy and relaxation, and help partners tune in to their bodies and each other.

SHARING ENERGY

The primary goal of the Sexual Mysteries is not the hoarding of energy, but the exchange of energy. Learning to pass energy back and forth with your partner is crucial. If you are not willing to do this, this book is a waste of your time. All of the rest of the exercises in this book involve the sharing of energy between partners.

Here is a simple exercise for learning to circulate energy with your partner. Sit facing your partner, either on the floor or in chairs. Hold your arms out in front of you, parallel to the floor, with your right palm down and your left palm up, and have your partner do the same. Place your palms on those of your partner.

Imagine energy (in whatever form you are most comfortable) flowing down your right arm and out through the palm of your right hand, and into your partner's left palm.

Once you can feel this, focus your attention on your left hand, and imagine your partner projecting energy into your left palm. Feel the energy traveling up your right arm, across your shoulders, and back down your right arm, to return to your partner. Your partner should imagine the same thing.

You can also increase the intensity of this exercise by using either synchronous or complementary breathing (described in Chapter Seven). Feel free to experiment with this exercise. You can vary your breathing, connect this circuit to various energy centers, or place various stones between your palms to see how this changes your ability to attune your energy with your partner's. (We've found that pyrite disks work well for this.)

Once you have mastered the above exercise, you can begin to practice doing the same thing during sex. Being aware of the energy flow between you and your partner is the next step. Once you can do this, you will be able to control the flow or direct it towards a specific purpose.

While making love, the man should focus on drawing energy down his spine, and then pushing it up into the woman as he thrusts into her. The woman should focus on pulling energy up her spine, and giving it back to him. The point of contact through which this is done will vary depending on the goal of your session.

If your goal is to stimulate or establish a connection between a particular energy center or point on the body, press those parts of the body together and imagine the energy flowing from the woman to the man at this point.

The current/polarity can be reversed as well. In this case, the man should focus on pulling energy up his spine and projecting it into the woman. The woman should focus on receiving this energy from the man, running it down her spine, and projecting it out of her vagina and into the man. It is important to become proficient with both polarities for these reasons:

- The ability to reverse the current allows you to experience the other partner's energy configuration, and gives insight into their side of the experience.

- The ability to reverse the current requires a refinement of your control over energy and thereby increases your skill at directing energy towards a specific goal.

- The ability to run energy either way gives you greater flexibility in both your spiritual and magical practices, as each part of the circuit requires a different mindset.

DIRECTING ENERGY THROUGH THE CENTERS

This exercise is described using the third eye center, but can be done with any energy center you desire.

Lie in a comfortable position, facing each other. Place your third eyes together, close your eyes, and begin breathing synchronously. On the inhale, one person brings energy up from their root center to their third eye; the other person draws energy in through the third eye connection and brings it down the spine to exit through the genitals, into the first person. Continue through several cycles of breathing.

When you have done this, you can try switching to complementary breathing. Trade roles, so you are familiar with both directions of energy flow. Once you've mastered this, try it while making love (at first, you won't want to distract yourself by moving during this exercise).

CONNECTING THE ENERGY CENTERS

This exercise can also be done with any energy center. Position yourself as described for the previous exercise. Use complementary breathing, so that as each person inhales, the other is exhaling, and vice versa. As each of you inhales, visualize energy coming into that energy center from your partner. As each of you exhales, visualize energy flowing out into your partner's energy center from yours. Continue through several cycles of breathing.

WOMAN ON TOP

Many of the traditional Tantric positions place the woman on top, for a very good reason. This is a powerful position for the woman. It gives her control over not only the physical aspects of sex (depth of penetration, tempo, degree of movement), but also over the flow of energy.

The man should either sit or lie down, whichever is more comfortable. The woman should straddle him, inserting his penis into her vagina. She can either move gently or remain still during this exercise. Again, breathing can be either synchronous or complementary.

The woman should imagine pulling energy up out of the man, drawing it up her spine, and then returning it to him in one of three ways. She can:

- Allow it to fountain out of her crown center and shower down onto him, or
- Allow it to flow back down her spine and into him through their genital connection, or
- Place her palms on some part of his body and allow it to flow down her arms and into him.

The man should focus on pushing energy up into the woman through the genital connection and receiving it in a way that is appropriate for whichever method the woman has chosen to return it.

Orgasm

Intense orgasms can be cathartic, and can make a person laugh, cry, faint, or even become nauseated. As a lover, it is important for you not to take these reactions personally. These are simply emotions and feelings coming to the surface, and are not necessarily a reflection of how your partner feels about you.

Orgasm: The Goat

To have a really strong, grounding orgasm (a "Goat" orgasm), breathe through your nose and mouth and move rapidly and forcefully, grasping your partner tightly and moaning or vocalizing loudly during orgasm. Imagine the orgasm exploding downwards through your body from the top of your head and into your partner.

Orgasm: The Star

To have an ethereal, "heavenly" orgasm (a "Star" orgasm), breathe deeply and as slowly as possible through the mouth. Try to relax your body as much as possible, and as orgasm approaches, vocalize dreamily in a slow, soft, drawn-out way: "Ohhhhhhhhh, aaaaaaaaah." When orgasm comes, imagine it as a wave that floods upwards through your body.

Orgasm: The Sky Father and the Earth Mother

The type of orgasm associated with Sky Father and Earth Mother consciousness depends upon learning to prolong arousal, and if you are male, to delay orgasm. Prolonging arousal helps you to satisfy your partner more thoroughly, gives you the freedom to enjoy the sexual act for longer periods of time, and offers an opportunity to have several orgasms in a single session. It gives you time to work with your own orgasmic energies, and allows you to begin controlling and directing the flow of energy through your body.

These exercises require a greater amount of control on the part of the male. A woman can continue to have sex after orgasm, but the man must attempt to refrain from ejaculating until the exercise is finished. It is crucial that involuntary ejaculation not be treated as a disappointment. Any of these exercises, performed for any length of time, will be beneficial, and they can always be repeated at the next session. Pleasure is a gift—appreciate it when it comes. Women, if your partner ejaculates before an exercise is finished, understand that he is learning, and appreciate the compliment (after all, he is having difficulty controlling himself while having sex with you). Men, satisfy your partner with whatever technique she prefers (manual, oral, or with a vibrator), and then enjoy the extra time you have to talk, snuggle, or play.

It is easier for women to learn how to have a whole-body orgasm through prolonged arousal than for men, so we focus below on techniques for the man, who must be able to delay ejaculation in order to sustain a state of prolonged arousal. Women should use the same techniques of slow movement, deep breathing, and the pulling of orgasmic energy up into the rest of the body.

To delay ejaculation, it is important to vary the rhythm and intensity of your thrusts. Many people believe that the most intense sexual pleasure comes from the most intense thrusts, and are surprised to find that even very slow movements can be extremely enjoyable, if you are paying close attention.

As a man's orgasm draws near, he may have the urge to stop thrusting to prevent ejaculation. Unfortunately, this can sometimes have the effect of triggering ejaculation, and the orgasm is usually very dissatisfying. If this is the case, the man should try changing his pace and intensity regularly rather than thrusting steadily, then stopping completely.

Another method of delaying ejaculation is bringing the energy of an impending orgasm upwards and backwards, up the spine. Men should imagine a channel in their pelvis corresponding to the placement of the vagina in women (this channel exists in the energetic body, but men don't usually notice it). During sex, the man should imagine that he is feeling the same sensations as his partner. As the man penetrates the woman, he should try to imagine her sensations of being penetrated mixing with his own, and imagine the energy flowing upwards in this channel. As orgasm approaches, the man should breathe deeply and slowly and increase the speed of his thrusts but reduce their length by pressing his groin tightly against the vagina and alternately tensing each buttock. This results in a circular, grinding sort of motion. During this motion, the orgasmic sensation will rise upward in the channel, activating the star-tide. Vocalizing (moaning, for instance) at this time intensifies the pleasurable sensation and may help the orgasm to rise.

Once a man succeeds in this technique, he may become quite enamored of the sensations that arise. As a result, beginners may actually pursue the whole-body orgasm too much. Take a break from this sort of work, and concentrate on ejaculatory orgasms until you feel more balanced. And remember, whole-body orgasms are not better than regular male orgasms. What is better is knowing how to do both. As a man becomes able to control his ejaculation, it becomes possible to have sex without ejaculating at all. Although this is often advocated in Eastern Tantra, these people were, frankly, playing a different game, seeking immortality rather than enlightenment. Listen to your body. Don't deny yourself ejaculations when your body needs them.

INVOKING DEITIES AND ARCHETYPES

In Chapter Four, we discussed invoking (or channeling) deities. This exercise can be performed during sex as well, and is worth exploring. Partners should try bringing different combinations of consciousness together to see what happens. In addition, it is possible for a partner to

help you invoke a deity. For instance, a woman may play the part of a Star goddess to help a man channel the Goat, because these archetypes are complementary and attract each other.

The Star prepares the room by lighting incense, lowering the lighting and putting some appropriate music on. The Goat meanwhile washes and grooms himself. When both are done, she then invites the Goat in, who makes some sort of offering to her. This can be a physical object, such as a flower or some small gift, but he may instead offer to brush her hair, give her a massage, or read a poem he has written or found. The Star appreciates the offering, then examines the Goat. As he stands still, she walks around him, looking him over and touching him. She imagines what their bodies can do together. She does nothing to make him nervous, such as making sudden moves or touching him in a rough way. The Goat remains very still, watching her as she does this, knowing that if he is accepted, he will be given the chance to make love to her.

She leads him to bed, where they lie against each other, practicing complementary breathing. Aroused, they begin kissing and stroking one another. The Goat focuses on the scent of her body, the feel of her flesh. The Star imagines how they look together, and contemplates each touch for its hidden meaning. When the Goat is satisfied that she is ready, he enters her. He directs his energies downward, into her, while she receives these and directs them upwards. They keep their eyes open, looking at each other, and thinking about how the other must feel. As he tunes into her, he senses what her body needs. She, swept by the waves of pleasure, begins to lose track of the difference between them. As they experience each other, there is a sense of merging; he can feel her feelings, and she can feel his. In this state of consciousness, they both approach orgasm.

ANOINTING YOUR PARTNER

If you are practicing with condoms for birth control or to avoid the risk of sexually-transmitted disease, skip this exercise entirely.

After sex, anoint each other's energy centers with your combined sexual fluids, using a clockwise motion. If you wish, you can also visualize closing or sealing the centers, which usually open during sex.

You can also use your combined sexual fluids to anoint each other ritually. This helps to break the social taboo of sexual fluids as "dirty," and also serves as a symbolic marking of the bond between you and your partner. When done ritualistically, with the understanding that this anointing is a divine gift, this simple action can take on a very serious or solemn nature. (Of course, if it turns into a finger-painting session, just enjoy it).

SLOWDOWN SEX

This can be an effective way of inducing a trance during sex. Once the man has begun thrusting, he should begin to slow the tempo, until he is hardly moving at all. As the woman moves to meet his thrusts, she should also slow down to match his speed. As your lovemaking slows down, slow your breathing too, until you are breathing slowly and deeply. Relax into the feeling.

MULTIPLE SESSION SEX

This exercise has a number of benefits, the primary being a refocusing of attention. Rather than stressing orgasm, it emphasizes the practice of sex for pleasure. Many of our society's sexual taboos are focused on non-reproductive sex (oral sex, anal sex, masturbation) and much of our sexual guilt comes from anxiety about this type of sex.

Sex without ejaculation can also change your definition of sex. For the man, it can make sex more sensual, and focus his attention on giving and receiving pleasure and affection. For the woman, it can allow her to understand the ways in which the male sex drive interacts with her own.

Often, women will find this type of sex very disconcerting at first, because they tend to measure sex by the performance of their partner: when he ejaculates, the lovemaking is over. When a woman has sex with a partner who chooses not to ejaculate, she may find that she is unsure exactly when to stop. She may not be used to the idea of participating in the decision to conclude the lovemaking session. Persistent practice will gradually overcome her concern.

To do this exercise, make love for a while. Before the man ejaculates (both of you may orgasm as many times as you like), stop and do something else for half an hour to an hour, either together or alone. This is an especially good time to meditate or do something creative, but do NOT do anything that will create a great deal of stress, like work, housecleaning, doing your taxes, etc. After that time, make love again. This time, the man ejaculates. As you become more proficient (and as your schedules permit), you can add more than one interlude to this exercise.

If the man ejaculates sooner than desired, don't get upset or let it spoil the session. He should simply satisfy the woman manually or orally (or any other way the couple desires).

Unless you are very advanced at energy work, do not attempt to wait more than an hour before making love the second time. It is difficult to hold onto a charge for long periods of time, and doing so can lead to mood swings, anger, resentment, energetic imbalance, and physical and emotional burnout. The energy must be either discharged or transmuted before this happens.

This technique can also be used as a means of building up energy for a magical act, but be warned that the energy built up during sex will be discharged during the magical act, and you may not want to continue your lovemaking later. If your partner is not completely willing to participate in your magical practice this way he or she may feel used, and harbor a great deal of anger and resentment towards you.

MELTING SEX

Once you have spent some time practicing passing energy back and forth during sex, you can try melting sex. This exercise is easier if you are already in a trance state when you begin, but can sometimes be achieved spontaneously. Melting sex is tricky, because it requires a tremendous amount of trust and the ability to temporarily turn off the part of you that protects your sense of individuality.

Once your lovemaking has begun, lie in any position that allows a great deal of skin-to-skin contact. Move slowly, imagining that you are melting into one another. First your energy fields begin to merge, then your bodies follow, until you are one pool of liquid.

Concentrate on the feeling of currents flowing through you, on the feeling of being liquid rather than solid. Is there anything "swimming"

in this pool? Don't worry about not being able to separate and become yourselves again. You will, and all too soon.

MOTIONLESS SEX

This type of sex can be performed in any position, although traditional Tantra usually recommends that it be done in a woman on top position. The most popular variation is the yab-yum position, where the man sits in full-lotus and the woman sits in his lap. If you are flexible enough to achieve this position without injury, feel free to try it, but if you are not, don't worry—it's not essential. The yab-yum position does, however, have two advantages: It places the woman on top, giving her greater control over the flow of energy, and it virtually immobilizes both partners, making it easier for both of you to avoid the temptation to seek stimulation through friction.

Engage in foreplay until both partners are ready for penetration, then assume a comfortable position (one you can remain in for ten minutes or more) and insert the penis into the vagina. Remain motionless, visualizing the energy flow (it doesn't matter who is running their energy up and who is running it down, as long as you form a complete circuit).

Once the energy flow has been visualized, both partners should begin short, fast PC contractions. Use the contractions to pump the energy through your bodies. Breathe deeply and slowly. You may either place your foreheads together at the third eye or gaze into each other's eyes. This exercise can be very tiring on more than just a physical level, so start off slowly and work up to longer sessions.

INITIATORY SEX

Initiatory sex can be empowering for both partners. The person being initiated will experience sex in a new way, and the person doing the initiating often develops a much deeper respect for their own sexuality. This simple but powerful exercise is excellent for someone who has been sexually abused in the past, especially if they are playing the part of the initiate. Set aside a couple of hours for this one—you will want to be able to take your time, and to have the freedom afterwards to deal with any emotions that may be raised by this exercise.

The initiator makes love to the initiate as if the initiate were a virgin. The initiate should express any hesitation or fears about anything that the initiator is doing, and the initiator should listen to those fears with concern, and then lovingly reassure the initiate before proceeding slowly, gently, and with a great deal of tenderness.

The initiate's role is to experience sex as if this were the first time. The initiator controls this situation, deciding what happens, while the initiate gives complete trust to the initiator and opens his or her mind to the sexual experience as if it were completely new.

SEX DURING MENSTRUATION

Sex during menstruation is taboo in many cultures, because it is considered "gross" or unclean, because women are ashamed of the fact that they are bleeding, and because of superstitions that have survived from earlier times when the energetics of menstruating women were only partially understood. It is said that a woman's power is strongest during menstruation, but this is not exactly true. Her *awareness* of energy flow is strongest at this time, and this makes it easier for her to control that energy.

In addition, a menstruating woman's naturally dominant tide shifts during menstruation. The normally dominant upward (celestial) flow is weakened, while the weaker downward (terrestrial) flow becomes stronger. This reversal is the basis of many of the taboos that prohibit sex with a menstruating woman: because the woman's energy flow has reversed and has assumed the terrestrial configuration, the man's energetic flow will tend to shift to complement it, and his energy flow will assume a celestially-dominant configuration. The taboo against menstruation arises from a deep male fear that taking on a traditionally-feminine energy configuration will make him feminine or effeminate, or will somehow make him less of a man. In fact, sex with a menstruating women, when performed with careful awareness, can bring a man into greater empathy with his partner and give him a greater understanding and appreciation of her needs and abilities, as well as helping him to tap into strengths that he has been taught to ignore or repress.

A woman who has practiced many of the exercises described in this book will also have the skill to reverse energy flow consciously. When learning to reverse energy flow, you might want to make a point to deliberately schedule the appropriate exercises during the woman's period, as it will make it easier for both of you to get the energy going in the right direction.

The type of sex that a woman will enjoy during menstruation may differ from the kinds of things she likes during the rest of her cycle. Some will prefer that it be gentler and dreamier, to help balance out the stronger earth-tide in them, while others will want to take advantage of the earth-tide, and be primal and wild.

SEXUAL POSITIONS

Descriptions of many sexual positions and their potential health benefits can be found in traditional Eastern Tantric texts, and we will not try to catalog them here. It is our firm belief that position and technique are not nearly as important as intent. You don't need to study a lot of sexual positions and formulae as long as you are willing to develop a sensitivity to your partner's energy flow and the skill to direct your own energy flow. Be familiar with various positions. As you progress, your intuition will begin to guide you in using them.

NINE

Sexual Rites

Throughout history, humans have used the energies of sexual union in ritualized ways. Two ancient forms of sexual ritual are the Sacred Marriage and Sacred Prostitution. In recent times, ritual sex has been practiced as a folk custom, and has also been used by such varied groups as Wiccans and Thelemic magicians, among others. It is apparent, upon examination of these traditions, that these modern practices differ in important ways from the ancient uses of sexual ritual.

Sacred Marriage

The oldest form of ritual sex known to us today is the Sacred Marriage (or *hieros gamos*). As ancient cultures began to develop and perfect the art of agriculture, they began to practice this rite. The sacred marriage was a fertility rite in which the current king of the land would publicly copulate with the high priestess, who represented the Goddess in her Earth Mother aspect. By joining with the king, the Earth Mother, through her priestess, demonstrated that he was her consort. This guaranteed that his kingdom would possess her good favor, and that they would enjoy fertile land and an abundant harvest. The king, in turn, became infused with the wisdom of the goddess' consort, giving him the wisdom he needed to rule effectively. The particular consort invoked by the king varied with the prevailing circumstances. In times of strife, warrior goddesses would be appropriate to preserve the land, while in times of plenty, more gentle, creative goddesses would be called on. Thus, the purpose of the Sacred Marriage is to use the sexual union of a man and woman to align and unite human will and the physical world with divine will and the supernatural world. This practice faded, predictably enough, as the worship of these goddesses declined and these societies became more male-dominant. However, because this practice has a long history, it has made a strong impression on the collective consciousness. Even though the original purpose of this ritual was ultimately political in nature, it can be adapted by modern practitioners for the purpose of communicating with a particular divinity, to ask for guidance or blessing.

Sacred Prostitution

Sacred prostitution is where the Sexual Mysteries found their clearest expression, and where the Goat and the Star archetypes were found to be the strongest. Sacred prostitution was not concerned with the fertility of the land, but with the development of civilization. This type of ritual sex emerged during the period where animal husbandry was being integrated with agricultural practices. This was the time when men's role in reproduction was becoming a social role, and men were being integrated into civilization. Social roles were in flux during this period, as men's and women's roles were being redefined with respect to the division of labor and participation in family life. The ultimate goal of this ritual is the joining of male and female consciousness into a harmonious whole through sexual union.

There were two primary types of sacred prostitution: one-time prostitution, and long-term devotion to the goddess.[1] One-time prostitution was an initiation rite for women, in which a girl, upon reaching puberty, would go to the temple of the goddess (Ishtar or one of her counterparts) and sit outside, waiting for a stranger to make an offering to the goddess and then to deflower her. In Babylonia and some other Semitic cultures, no girl was allowed to marry until she had undergone this ritual. This type of prostitution initiated the maiden (the Star) into the Sexual Mysteries, giving her a taste of Earth Mother consciousness and preparing her for marriage. (However, the girl was not expected to officially assume the role of Earth Mother until she was married.) This rite was practiced in the Near East, and may have existed in Egypt.

It was very important, in this type of prostitution, that the girl be initiated by a stranger. This may seem strange to us—why wouldn't she want to be initiated by someone that she knew? The answer to this question lies in the nature of the Star, and her sexuality. The Star is completely independent, and free to choose her sexual contacts at will. No man has the right to control her, sexually or otherwise. Since it was important that the girl being initiated not be tied to her initiator, what better person than a stranger to fill this role?

The second type of sacred prostitution was performed by women who had devoted themselves to the service of the goddess. The sacred prostitute was a civilizing force. Men who came to her were bathed, fed, ritually anointed, sung to or otherwise entertained, and then made love to. This type of prostitution initiated the wild man (the Goat) into the

Sexual Mysteries, giving him a glimpse of Sky Father consciousness and encouraging him to take on the social roles required of him by urban civilization. These types of rites took place in Egypt, the Near East, and Greece, under the auspices of Hathor, Ishtar, Inanna, Astarte, Tanit, Artemis, and Aphrodite, and various other goddesses.

We see this function of the sacred prostitute as a force of civilization in the Sumerian myth of Ea-bani and Ukhat. Gilgamesh, the king of the city of Erech (a Sky Father) wishes to bring Ea-bani, a wild shepherd (a Goat), into the city as an ally. The king sends a hunter, Tsaidu, to capture Ea-bani, but the shepherd is both strong and wary, and cannot be caught. When Gilgamesh sees that Tsaidu is unsuccessful, he sends the woman Ukhat out after Ea-bani.

Ukhat seduces Ea-bani, and makes love to him for six days and six nights. When they are finished, Ea-bani looks for his herd and discovers that they have deserted him. Rather than chasing his flock, Ea-bani listens to Ukhat, who says:

> Thou art of great stature, O Ea-bani, and art like unto a god. Why then dost thou lie with the beasts of the field? Come, let me bring thee to strong-walled Erech....

Ea-bani, in love with Ukhat, agrees. He then adopts the mannerisms of civilization (the role of the Sky Father) and becomes Gilgamesh's most trusted companion.[2]

This second type of ritual prostitution survived well into the second or third century C.E., at which time it was overrun by the celibate philosophy of the early Church fathers. However, despite the anti-sexual efforts of early Christianity, marriage (which is, ideally, a ritual involving the initiation of the Goat and the Star into Earth Mother and Sky Father consciousness) is still considered to be the foundation of our civilization.

These types of ritual prostitution produced the states of consciousness that gave birth to the Sky Father and the Earth Mother—archetypes that shape our gender roles even today.

FOLK PRACTICES

Despite Christianity's denial of sexuality, many people still remembered the Sacred Marriage and the practice of Sacred Prostitution, and these rites evolved into the folk custom of coupling in the fields every spring to increase fertility and ensure a good harvest. No longer a means of communing with the gods, these sexual rites had evolved into a form of sympathetic magic practiced by farmers to influence the forces of nature on which they were dependent for sustenance. This practice survived until modern times in rural areas throughout Europe, despite official condemnation by the Church. Even in a sexually-restricted social climate, this ancient pattern still struggles to resurface.

THE GREAT RITE

Recently, a modified form of the Sacred Marriage was revived by Gerald Gardner, the founder of Wicca, in the ritual referred to as the Great Rite. In the Wiccan Great Rite, participants celebrate the union of polarities—of male and female, of sun and moon, of fire and water. The Great Rite is much more abstract than the *hieros gamos* practiced by ancient peoples. It is a highly symbolic religious ceremony which can be either celebratory or adapted towards a magical purpose. As public sex is not considered acceptable in modern times, the Great Rite is usually conducted in private, or is performed symbolically by submerging the blade of a knife (representing the phallus of the god) into a chalice of water or some other appropriate liquid (representing the womb of the goddess). In Wicca, the Great Rite is the third and final form of initiation, representing the transition from student to full member and entitling initiates to leave the coven and found their own. The Great Rite bears little resemblance to ancient practices in its details and its goals, and should be considered a new form of sexual ritual.

The Athame and Chalice in the Great Rite

THELEMIC SEX MAGIC

Aleister Crowley, founder of the modern tradition of Thelemic magic, also incorporated sexual magic into his workings, and his ninth, tenth, and eleventh level initiations involved autoerotic, heterosexual, and homosexual activity. Crowleyan sex magic excels at making use of the energy released by breaking sexual taboos (which were plentiful during the Victorian era, but scarce in ancient times). Predictably, it bears little resemblance to the ancient practices discussed in this book, but it is a highly effective means of liberating repressed or blocked sexual energy, which, once freed, can be directed towards magical goals.

THE SEXUAL MYSTERIES

If you wanted to enact the Sacred Marriage as it was practiced in ancient times, it would be very easy to pick the culture you feel most comfortable with, and to duplicate (in some cases, word for word) the rituals that culture practiced. However, literally re-creating the Sacred Marriage would be, at best, a religious celebration that makes clear the mindset of an agricultural people whose lives were deeply connected to the earth. At worst, the Sacred Marriage would be time spent going through the motions of a ceremony that no longer holds meaning for us.

You could also attempt to practice Sacred Prostitution, but there are many reasons having sex with strangers is a bad idea in modern society.

How can we use these rites today? The energetics underlying these two rituals are the key to doing this. Sacred Marriage was a way of receiving divine guidance and good will. We can do this today by invoking deities within us for the benefit and instruction of our partners. Sacred prostitution was a way of introducing men and women to new ways of being. Today, women can initiate men into the Sky Father role by invoking the Earth Mother within themselves. Men can initiate women into the Earth Mother state by invoking the Sky Father within themselves. Also, men can initiate women into Star-consciousness by being the Goat, and women can initiate men into Goat-consciousness by being the Star. In other words, sex can be used to put us in touch with our shadow sides, and allow us to integrate the disconnected parts of our beings into a harmonious whole.

SACRED SEXUALITY IN A RITUAL CONTEXT

Our modern world makes certain details of ancient sexual practice unfeasible or difficult. However, it is possible to immerse ourselves into the same pools of consciousness in which our ancestors bathed if we realize that the details are just that—details. We can find paths to these states of being that are appropriate to our times.

For this reason, we do not describe anywhere in this book a specific ritual to be followed. Ritual is a very personal thing, and each ritual must be tailored specifically to your intent. Instead, we outline a basic structure for ritual sex, describe a few possible scenarios, and offer a number of guidelines that will help you design rituals that are appropriate for you.

Before you design your ritual, ask yourself what you are trying to achieve. Every detail of your ritual will be determined by the goal you have set for yourself. Without a specific purpose, any ritual you design is likely to fail.

Once you have chosen a goal or purpose, think about how it can best be achieved. Do you want to invoke a specific set of deities? Make a point to get to know them first, through mythological research and meditation upon the descriptions you find.

Designing Your Own Ritual

A good ritual has five basic steps:

- Creation of sacred space
- Focusing of awareness
- The raising of power
- The discharge or transmutation of power
- Closing the space

Each of these steps plays an important part in your ritual, and removing or changing the order of any of these elements will make your ritual less effective. Any celebration or socializing should be done either before the ritual has begun or after the sacred space has been closed.

Step One: Creation of Sacred Space

Why do we need to create sacred space? In order to successfully perform any magical or consciousness-altering ritual, you must put yourself into a state of mind that is very receptive to outside influences. It is important to be sure that the only influences you will be exposed to within your sacred space are positive ones. Creating sacred space involves securing the area in which you will be working. It is important to be completely focused on what you are doing. If you need to worry about being interrupted or having to deal with mundane details, you will not be able to attain the necessary level of focus. If you already have a preferred method of creating sacred space, such as casting a circle, feel free to use it. Creating sacred space can include such steps as cleaning the area to be used, ritually purifying it with incense, sprinkling the edges of the space with salt water, or simply visualizing a circle or sphere of white light around your selected space before beginning.

Step Two: Focusing or Grounding of Awareness

The second step of ritual is to focus your awareness on the task at hand, clearing it of all other details. This is the stage at which you crystallize your intent, and then, by inducing a trance state, create the state of consciousness appropriate to the goal of your ritual. You can crystallize your intent by meditation on it, by formally stating it aloud, or by symbolizing it in a ritual action. Once you have done this, induce trance by whichever method you find most effective and appropriate. Common methods include dancing or other types of movement, chanting, singing, drumming, breathing exercises, meditation, masturbation or sexual activity.

If you are invoking any deities during your ritual, this is the time to do it. Just remember that deities are not dogs—they do not necessarily come when they are called. If the deities you invoked choose to be present, they will appear at a time that they feel is appropriate.If others appear instead, be flexible.

Step Three: The Raising of Power

Raising power can occur either during or after trance induction. Most of the trance induction methods listed above can also be used to raise power, but if you feel that you have not raised enough power to complete the task at hand, feel free to use any exercise or visualization that you find helpful. If you are not already engaged in love-making, begin now.

Step Four: The Discharge of Power

This is the climax of the ritual—the point at which the power that has been raised is actually used to accomplish the goal of your ritual. In a sexual ritual, this occurs at orgasm. If you have reached the stage where you are multi-orgasmic, this step can last for quite a while.

Step Five: Closing the Space

Now that your ritual has been accomplished, it is time to tie up any loose ends (emotional or otherwise) before ending. Make offerings to any deities who may have been present or whom you wish to honor, thank any entities who may have assisted you (including your partner), and meditate on what you've just experienced. These things will not only help you assimilate anything that may have happened, but will also let your subconscious mind know that the ritual is over, and that you are returning to the mundane world. You may choose, at this point, to deliberately break whatever trance you have achieved, or to remain in that state until it slowly wears off. This is really a matter of personal preference.

RITUAL TOOLS

You may prefer to incorporate magical tools (wands, chalices, etc.) from your existing practices into your sex rituals. Tools can serve as a focus, either by helping you to maintain your concentration on your goal or by making it easier to carry out ritual actions. But there is no magical tool, other than your body, that you cannot do without. In fact, there are times when a magical tool can be a distraction from what you are trying to do with your body. Keep it simple.

PLANNING YOUR RITUAL

You can be as spontaneous or structured about your ritual as you like. If you feel the need to plan every detail ahead of time, go ahead. Just be flexible if things don't happen exactly the way you expect them to. If you are also writing speeches to be recited during your ritual, be sure to memorize them. If you are struggling to remember the words, you won't be able to focus on the ritual itself.

Ritual can also be completely spontaneous, as long as you have an understanding of the ritual structure described above. Start by sitting for a few minutes, focusing on the intent of your ritual. When you have that goal clearly in mind, look through your tools and pick up anything that seems to speak to you. When intuition tells you that you have what you need, return to your ritual space, arrange whatever objects you may have chosen as seems appropriate, and let your ritual be guided by whatever tools you have chosen. You may surprise yourself with this method—often you will find yourself doing things with the tools that you've never done before, without having thought about it beforehand. Spontaneous ritual is extremely difficult to do with a partner, as it requires that you both be perfectly attuned to each other, but it is possible. Don't force it—when you?re ready for it, it will happen.

RITUAL SCENARIOS

Rather than spelling out a specific ritual, we prefer to describe basic ritual structure and offer some possible ritual scenarios for you to adapt for your own use. These scenarios are merely possibilities. Feel free to alter them as you like, or make up your own. These scenarios will help you to experience the Sexual Mysteries in ways that are similar to the rites in which those mysteries were first solidified, but, of course, there are countless paths to the mysteries. If you do choose to build a ritual around one of these scenarios, realize that the details are quite flexible. You can add any that seem appropriate to you and omit any that are unsuited to your situation. Just be guided by the spirit of the scenario.

Either of these roles can be played by either partner, and we encourage you to experience both roles. The terms Satyr and Nymph, Sky Father and Earth Mother, etc., are used only because they conjure up the specific feeling you want to achieve with the scenario. Do not hesitate to adapt the characters to your own personal style, or to change the names if these make you feel uncomfortable.

The Hierodule Scenario: Initiation into Celestial Consciousness

One of you will play the role of the Hierodule, or sacred prostitute; the other will play the part of the Stranger. After sacred space has been created and a trance state has been induced, the Stranger approaches the Hierodule, and the Hierodule greets the Stranger, offering him or her hospitality. The Stranger accepts, and allows the Hierodule to ritually

bathe,[3] feed, massage, and/or entertain them (by singing, dancing, reading poetry, etc.) as sensually as possible. When the Stranger has been refreshed, he or she offers the Hierodule a small gift. (This can be later offered or consecrated to the deities of your choice, and kept for use by both partners in future rituals.) The Hierodule accepts the gift, and initiates lovemaking. When lovemaking is complete, the Hierodule blesses the Stranger, and together they make a small offering to the appropriate deities. The Stranger then leaves.

The Satyr Scenario: Initiation into Terrestrial Consciousness

This scenario lends itself least to a ritual format, but can be conducted as such if you are willing to set up a loose structure and be spontaneous within that structure. One of you will play the role of the Satyr, and the

other will play the role of the Nymph. After the sacred space has been created and a trance has been induced, the Nymph approaches the Satyr, who is engaged in some sort of sensual activity (dancing, playing music, singing). The Satyr invites the Nymph to join him, and she agrees. The Satyr engages the Nymph in some sort of playful activity (dancing, singing, making daisy crowns, smelling flowers, reading poetry, or playing a silly physically oriented game like leap-frog). The Satyr may pretend to be an animal or talk to her in silly voices—he wants to make the Nymph laugh. Once the Nymph is completely relaxed, the Satyr seduces her, making love to her slowly and gently, as if she were a virgin. The Nymph surrenders completely to the Satyr, allowing him to do anything with her that he desires. He does. When the love-making is complete, the Satyr gives the Nymph a small token of his affection (a flower, a pretty leaf, a small rock) and sends her on her way. If an offering to any particular deity is desired, it can be done before the Nymph departs.

The Sacred Marriage Scenario: Acknowledging the Earth Mother and the Sky Father

This scenario lends itself to a much more formal ritual than the first two. One of you will play the part of the King (the Sky Father), and the other will play the part of the Priestess (the Earth Mother), or the parts of King and Priestess can be switched for Queen and Priest. After sacred space has been created and you have induced a trance state, the Priestess invokes the deity of her choice, and the King approaches the Priestess. He formally declares his reverence for the goddess she represents, and asks for her blessing. The Priestess indicates to the King that he may approach her, and they move to the bed. This can be a small space that signifies the sacred marriage bed, and can be as simple as a blanket that has been laid on the ground and perfumed or strewn with flower petals. The King makes love to the Priestess reverently, worshipping her with his body. When the love-making is complete, the Priestess blesses the King, assuring him of her good will and promising him future assistance. Together they make an offering to the appropriate deity before leaving.

The Elemental Scenario: Attuning to Nature

This scenario is best conducted as an outdoor ritual, but if circumstances make this impossible, it can still be done effectively indoors. One of you will play the role of Gaia (or the Earth Mother of your choice), and the other will play the role of Ouranos (or the Sky Father of your choice). Find a suitable spot outside, or clear away a large space in your ritual room. After sacred space has been created and you have induced a trance state, Gaia and Ouranos are invoked. Gaia focuses on her terrestrial nature, visualizing her body as the earth, the curves of her body forming mountains and valleys. Ouranos focuses on his celestial nature, visualizing his body as the sky, the warmth of his body becoming the sun and the breath of his body becoming the wind. When they are both ready, they make love to each other. His caresses are the sun and the rain caressing the earth, her kisses are the flowers reaching up to catch the breeze as it brushes by. When lovemaking is complete, they separate. In this scenario, the lovemaking itself is an offering to the Earth Mother and Sky Father deities you have chosen to represent.

RITUAL GUIDELINES

Here are some guidelines that will help your rituals to flow smoothly:

- Once the ritual has begun, do NOT interrupt it with social chatter or any conversation that is not directly related to your goal. If you wish to add any steps to this ritual, add them before the ritual begins or after power has been discharged. Inserting them anywhere else will break the rhythm of the ritual and dissipate whatever energy has been raised.

- Have everything you need handy so that you don't have to fumble with it or stop to look for it. If you are using birth control, be sure to apply it beforehand or have it within reach. There is a theory in some pagan circles that "if the Great Rite is performed correctly, there is no chance of pregnancy, as the creative forces will be directed elsewhere." Even if this is true, it is foolish to risk possible pregnancy as a consequence of a lapse in concentration during ritual.

• Be prepared. If you are going to be memorizing an invocation, make sure you know it by heart.

• Pick a time and place where you are certain you will not be interrupted. If possible, schedule your ritual at a time where you will have nothing to do afterward but meditate, write, or sleep. Eliminate as many distractions as possible. Lock the door, unplug the phone, and, if necessary, block out external sounds with music.

• If you want to use pre-recorded music, put your CD player on repeat or play your tape in a stereo that will automatically flip sides. The last thing you want to do is get up to re-start the music. Be careful in your selection of music—you are going to be listening to it in an extremely vulnerable state of mind, and you don't want to imprint an unwanted message in the course of your ritual.

• Be flexible. The deities you invoke may have different ideas about what should occur in ritual than you do, and once they have arrived, you may discover that what you have planned is not appropriate. Let them act through you as they will. They can teach you much more than you could learn by sticking to a pre-designed ritual.

• Know your deities. Be sure that the deities you've invoked are the right ones for whatever you want to do or learn. You should also make sure that the deity you choose to tune in is compatible with the one your partner wishes to focus on. Never try to combine deities who were antagonistic to each other in their respective mythologies. Studying the customs and mythologies surrounding a deity will help you to avoid any serious mistakes.

• Be spontaneous. Choreographed sex is appropriate to erotic films, but not to this sort of ritual. Feel free to incorporate any of the techniques described in this book, but never at the expense of the flow of the ritual.

- Leave your relationship out of the ritual. During the ritual, you are not a couple—you are two magical practitioners working towards a common goal. This is neither the time nor the place for critical comments, discussion of personal problems, or the attempted resolution of an ongoing fight. If you are fighting, resolve the fight and make up before conducting any sort of sexual ritual.

- After the ritual is completed, you may wish to write about it in your journal or sit quietly for a bit and contemplate what has occurred, observing any changes in your state of mind. You may want to avoid talking about the ritual immediately afterwards, for two reasons. First, you may find yourself tempted to analyze the experience, dissecting it before you have a chance to assimilate it on a mystical or intuitive level. Second, you will have accumulated a certain amount of creative energy that will be dissipated in conversation rather than drawn on for inspiration.

- It's good to be eclectic. Just be sure that you are combining elements that work together, rather than working against each other. Respect the cultures from which you are borrowing. Eclecticism is not a ruthless appropriation of others' customs, but a respectful, appreciative integration of those customs into your own personal practice.

Sacred sexuality is always a matter of using the connection of physical bodies to create a connection of consciousnesses. Ritual is a means of focusing the will on a particular goal or desire. Combining the two is a way of deliberately using sex to achieve a goal.

Modern sexuality and sex magic can get very complex because of anti-sexual societal influences. Ancient sexuality, while simpler and more direct, can be very hard to duplicate in its details. By understanding the mechanics of ritual, and by understanding the underlying goal of sexual rituals, it is possible to create your own rituals that are personally appropriate and meaningful.

ENDNOTES

1. There was, of course, profane prostitution occurring at this time as well. However, it was practiced outside of a religious context and has nothing to do with the mysteries we are discussing here.

2. *Babylonian Religion and Mythology, vol. 4,* Leonard William King, AMS Press, New York, 1976.

3. If bathing the whole body is impractical, a foot bath is a nice substitute.

Afterword

The Sexual Mysteries consist of three endeavors: Living, Loving, and Learning. Living is about self-knowledge: liberating your shadow-self, understanding how your mind and body operate, and having an awareness of how you are connected to the rest of the world. Loving is about sharing yourself and your discoveries with others, and about creating new realities and ways of being by joining together with others. Learning is about giving and receiving knowledge, and applying it to your life. As we learn, we change how we live, and the cycle goes on and on. This simple idea can be very difficult to practice in a world where consciousness has been fragmented, and where the expression of love is strongly limited by social pressures. For this reason, communicating with people who are trying to live in the same way can be helpful. However, finding others with truly similar interests is a constant problem in the world today, especially when one's interests contradict so many widespread cultural beliefs.

As discussed in Chapter Four, consciousness connects us all. It is a means for us to make connections with people who have similar beliefs, even if they are not physically present. If you are ever alone and need to talk to someone about your experiences with the Sexual Mysteries, you may try to connect, on the level of consciousness, with all of the people in the world who are doing the same. Some of them may have answers for you. Similarly, you may wish to make your own wisdom available to others.

To make this process easier, we have included a symbol at the end of this book that can be used as a gateway to the Sexual Mysteries. Symbols are important ways of guiding one in the world of consciousness, for they act like addresses in the physical world. In other words, a symbol is something that points to a "place" in consciousness. By focusing your attention on a symbol, you make a connection with a certain area of consciousness.

If you contemplate an image while thinking about something, it becomes easier for another person to access those thoughts if they also contemplate the same image. Using this process, we, the authors, have linked our insights to the gateway symbol. We will continue to do so as we learn more. If you have a realization you wish to share, we encourage you to do the same: contemplate the symbol, and think about your insight. Conversely, if you have a question or concern, you may contemplate the symbol to connect with this growing pool of information. Realize that the information may manifest itself consciously, or at some deeper level, as an experience that will give you your answer.

The symbol is composed of two concentric circles, enclosing a hexagram made from two overlapping equilateral triangles. Within the

Connecting Symbol of the Sexual Mysteries

hexagram is an eye, composed of a *vesica pisces* (a shape formed by the intersection of two circles that each touch the center point of the other) and a smaller circle within. This symbol is a reflection of the Sexual Mysteries. The outer circle represents the world and wholeness. The inner circle represents the Mysteries, as a reflection of wholeness and as a system for understanding it. The triangles of the hexagram represent celestial (upward-pointing)and terrestrial (downward-pointing) consciousness; the hexagram itself represents their joining. The eye represents three separate, but linked, ideas. First, it represents the self-aware consciousness that is created by the joining of the celestial and terrestrial. Second, it represents sexual union: the vesica pisces represents the vagina, while the circle represents the penis within. Third, the vesica pisces represents the joining of physical and spiritual reality: the circle within represents a seed that is growing, the seed of the new reality that comes when we remember that we are not only physical beings on a spiritual path, but spiritual beings on a physical path.

Recommended Reading

CONSCIOUSNESS

Future Memory: How Those Who "See the Future" Shed Light on the Workings of the Human Mind. P. M. H. Atwater. Birch Lane Press, 1996. Another book for opening the mind to new models of consciousness.

The Holographic Universe. Michael Talbot. Harper Perennial, 1991. A good introduction to new ways of conceptualizing the mind and reality.

The Holotropic Mind: The Three Levels of Human Consciousness and How They Shape Our Lives. Stanislav Grof, M.D., with Hal Zina Bennett. Harper San Francisco, 1993. An in-depth study of the holographic, transpersonal model of consciousness.

Goddesses in Every Woman and *Gods in Every Man.* Jean Shinoda Bolen, M.D. Harper Colophon Books, 1984. These books offer an excellent way to begin discovering which deities you are attuned to. While Dr. Bolen sticks to Greek mythology, her methods can be applied to any pantheon you like.

EASTERN TANTRA AND WESTERN SEXOLOGY

Ecstasy Through Tantra. Dr. Jonn Mumford. Llewellyn Publications, 1994. This overview of Eastern Tantra is a little bit compressed for beginners, but contains a great deal of information.

The Jewel in the Lotus: The Sexual Path to Higher Consciousness. Sunyata Saraswati and Bodhi Avinasha. Tantrika International, 1994. One of the best books on Tantric sexual techniques available. This one is a bit advanced for beginners.

Sexual Energy Ecstasy: A Practical Guide to Lovemaking Secrets of the East and West. David and Ellen Ramsdale. Peak Skill Publishing Inc., 1991. An outstanding presentation of Eastern Tantra for Western readers. This book is a tremendous resource, both for beginners and for advanced practitioners.

Sexual Secrets: The Alchemy of Ecstasy. Nik Douglas and Penny Slinger. Destiny Books, 1979. A valuable resource for anyone who has begun Tantric practice, and would like to begin delving into the Hindu and Taoist traditions.

ENERGY WORK AND HEALTH

Bodymind by Ken Dychtwald. G. P. Putnam's Sons, 1986. A fascinating in-depth discussion of the interaction of mind and body, with lots of practical information.

A Chakra and Kundalini Workbook: Psycho-Spiritual Techniques for Health, Rejuvenation, Psychic Powers and Spiritual Realization. Dr. Jonn Mumford. Llewellyn Publications, 1994. A complex but very useful series of chakra and kundalini exercises. You could take years going through this book, and the time would be well-spent.

Energize! The Alchemy of Breath and Movement for Health and Transformation. Elrond, Juliana, and Sophia Blawyn with Suzanne Jones. Llewellyn Publications, 1993. A collection of movement and meditation exercises from a wide variety of traditions, including yoga, tai chi, chi kung, and belly dancing.

Food for Thought: A New Look at Food and Behavior, Saul Miller with Jo Anne Miller. Prentice Hall Inc., 1979. A discussion of how food affects consciousness.

Hands of Light: A Guide to Healing Through the Human Energy Field. Barbara Ann Brennan. Bantam Books, 1988. A very detailed workbook for those wishing to learn basic energy work.

The Yoga of Herbs: An Ayurvedic Guide to Herbal Medicine. Dr. David Frawley and Dr. Vasant Lad. Lotus Press, 1988. An excellent presentation of Ayurvedic theory and herbalism. Extremely useful for anyone who is either already studying herbs or who would like to begin.

MYTHOLOGY

The Cults of the Greek States: Volumes 1–4. Lewis Richard Farnell, M.A. Aegaean Press, 1971. In-depth study of Greek mythology, organized by deity. This book is written for a very academic audience, but if you're interested in more than just Bullfinch's version of ancient mythology, it's fascinating.

The Greek Myths: Volumes 1 and 2. Robert Graves. Penguin Books, 1960. Summarizes variants of the main myths of Greek mythology An excellent starting point for research. Also easy to read, and written very poetically.

Inanna, Queen of Heaven and Earth: Her Stories and Hymns from Sumer. Diane Wolkstein and Samuel Noah Kramer. Harper and Row, 1983. Easy-to-read introduction to the original Sumerian stories about Inanna.

The New Larousse Encyclopedia of Mythology. trans. Richard Aldington and Delano Ames. Hamlyn Publishing Group, 1983. Offers a broad overview of the mythology of a number of ancient and modern cultures.

Stories from Ancient Canaan. trans. and ed. Michael David Coogan. The Westminster Press, 1978. Easy introduction to Canaanite mythology; includes synopses and interpretations of the Ugaritic texts.

The Witches' Goddess and The Witches' God. Janet and Stewart Farrar. Phoenix Publishing Inc., 1987. These books give a brief but excellent overview of various deities as they are seen by many Wiccans today.

The Woman's Encyclopedia of Myths and Secrets. Barbara G. Walker. Harper and Row Publishers, 1983. Contains a great deal of interesting information, as seen through a strongly feminist perspective on history.

SEX MAGICK

The Tree of Ecstasy: An Advanced Manual of Sexual Magic. Dolores Ashcroft-Nowicki. Aquarian Press, 1991. A wonderful book on pagan sexual ritual, including rites for each season. Can also be used as a starting point for designing your own rituals. For the more advanced student.

Secrets of Sex Magic: A Practical Handbook for Men and Women. Frater U. D. Llewellyn Publications, 1995. An excellent no-nonsense beginner's guide to sex magic practices.

Index

Ecstasy through Tantra
Dr. Jonn Mumford

Dr. Jonn Mumford makes the occult dimension of the sexual dynamic accessible to everyone. One need not go up to the mountaintop to commune with Divinity: its temple is the body, its sacrament the communion between lovers. *Ecstasy Through Tantra* traces the ancient practices of sex magick through the Egyptian, Greek and Hebrew forms, where the sexual act is viewed as symbolic of the highest union, to the highest expression of Western sex magick.

Dr. Mumford guides the reader through mental and physical exercises aimed at developing psychosexual power; he details the various sexual practices and positions that facilitate "psychic short-circuiting" and the arousal of Kundalini, the Goddess of Life within the body. He shows the fundamental unity of Tantra with Western Wicca, and he plumbs the depths of Western sex magick, showing how its techniques culminate in spiritual illumination. Includes 14 full-color photographs.

0-87542-494-5, 190 pp., 6 x 9, 14 color plates, softcover   **$16.00**

Astral Love
Romance, Ecstasy & Higher Consciousness
D. J. Conway

Performing sex magick on the astral plane is an advanced magickal technique, one of the most powerful that exists. Now this ancient esoteric knowledge—once reserved for the highest initiates—can be yours through the practical methods in *Astral Love*.

If you lack a reliable sex partner, astral sex can be a safe and fulfilling alternative which can lead to intense ecstasy. If your goal is to find a physical partner, your astral lover can help you locate the right person. Or if your relationship with your mate is lacking, an astral lover can satisfy many unfulfilled needs—without putting your primary relationship at risk.

Forging a personal relationship on the astral plane will enhance your life, filling it with love, compassion, understanding, and positive energy on all levels. Astral sex can even help you establish a stronger connection with the Divine and open new avenues of magick. Even if you choose not to be sexually active on the astral planes, you can establish strong, warm friendships with high-level beings to enhance your magick and advance spiritually. Learn how to safely travel to and enlist the help of the astral realm with this eminently practical guide.

1-56718-161-9, 192 pp., 6 x 9, illus., softcover $12.95

Dark Moon Mysteries
Wisdom, Power and Magick of the Shadow World
Timothy Roderick

You are a blend of balancing energies: masculine and feminine, active and passive, and light and dark. However, most books on spirituality and empowerment avoid addressing your psyche's native darker aspects—even though it's vital that you claim your "darkness" to becoming a whole, integrated, empowered person.

Dark Moon Mysteries is the first book to explore the "dark side" of spirit, ritual, symbol, psyche, and magic. It is also the first book on Witchcraft to make use of storytelling to access wisdom and insight, in the tradition of *Women Who Run with the Wolves*. This book weaves together Jungian analysis, the practical application of imagery from ancient fairy tales, and contemporary Witchcraft to help you come to grips with the darker shades of your being. You'll use magic, rituals, dance, guided journeys, and more to explore your deep consciousness.

Work spiritually and magically with the Dark Moon to touch upon the very source of your inner power and to move beyond your fears and limitations. Embrace all aspects of your psyche and follow the true path of the Witch, shaman, magician and mystic.

1-56718-345-X, 240 pp., 6 x 9, softcover $14.95

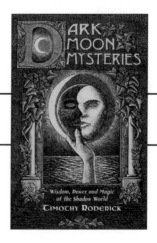

Maiden, Mother, Crone
The Myth and Reality of the Triple Goddess
D. J. Conway

The Triple Goddess is with every one of us each day of our lives. In our inner journeys toward spiritual evolution, each woman and man goes through the stages of Maiden (infant to puberty), Mother (adult and parent) and Crone (aging elder). *Maiden, Mother, Crone* is a guide to the myths and interpretations of the Great Goddess archetype and her three faces, so that we may better understand and more peacefully accept the cycle of birth and death.

Learning to interpret the symbolic language of the myths is important to spiritual growth, for the symbols are part of the map that guides each of us to the Divine Center. Through learning the true meaning of the ancient symbols, through facing the cycles of life, and by following the meditations and simple rituals provided in this book, women and men alike can translate these ancient teachings into personal revelations.

Not all goddesses can be conveniently divided into the clear aspects of Maiden, Mother and Crone. This book covers these others as well, including the Fates, the Muses, Valkyries and others.

0-87542-171-7, 240 pp., 6 x 9, softcover   **$12.95**

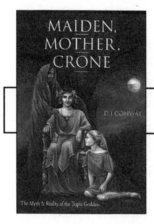

To order call 1-800-THE MOON
Prices subject to change without notice.

Lord of Light & Shadow
The Many Faces of the God
D. J. Conway

Early humans revered the great Goddess and all Her personalized aspects, but they also revered the God as Her necessary and important consort, lover, and son. *Lord of Light and Shadow* leads you through the myths of the world's diverse cultures to find the archetypal Pagan God hidden behind all of them. He is a being with the traits and aspects that women secretly desire in men, and that men desire to emulate. The patriarchal religions assimilated the ancient spirit of the Pagan God—in one form or another—into their scriptures. Yet, despite the deliberate changes to his identity, there is something about the God that could never be destroyed. By searching for the original Pagan God in these mythologies, you will find his spiritual essence and the path to the truth.

1-56178-177-5, 240 pp., 6 x 9, illus., softcover   **$14.95**

Magick of the Gods and Goddesses
How to Invoke Their Powers
(formerly titled *Ancient and Shining Ones*)
D. J. Conway

Magick of the Gods and Goddesses is a handy, comprehensive reference guide to the myths and deities from ancient religions around the world. Now you can easily find the information you need to develop your own rituals and worship using the Gods/Goddesses with which you resonate most strongly. More than just a mythological dictionary, Magick of the Gods and Goddesses explains the magickal aspects of each deity and explores such practices as Witchcraft, Ceremonial Magick, Shamanism and the Qabala. It also discusses the importance of ritual and magick, and what makes magick work.

Most people are too vague in appealing for help from the Cosmic Beings—they either end up contacting the wrong energy source, or they are unable to make any contact at all, and their petitions go unanswered. In order to touch the power of the universe, we must re-educate ourselves about the Ancient Ones. The ancient pools of energy created and fed by centuries of belief and worship in the deities still exist. Today these energies can bring peace of mind, spiritual illumination and contentment. On a very earthy level, they can produce love, good health, money, protection, and success.

1-56718-179-1, 448 pp., 7 x 10, 300 illus., softcover   **$17.95**

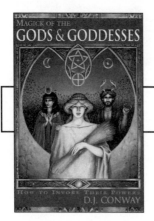

To order call 1-800-THE MOON
Prices subject to change without notice.

The New Book of Goddesses and Heroines
Patricia Monaghan

They come out in your dreams, your creativity, your passion, and in all of your relationships. They represent you in all your glory and complexity, and you represent them. They are the goddesses and heroines that form our true history. Your history. Let these mythic stories nourish your soul as they speak to you on a level as deep and mysterious as the source of life itself.

The third edition of this classic reference offers a complete, shining collection of goddess myths from around the globe. Discover more than 1,500 goddesses in Australia, Africa, North and South America, Asia, Europe—and experience Her as She truly is. This new edition also adds hundreds of new entries to the original text—information found only in rare or limited editions and obscure sources.

There is a new section named "Cultures of the Goddess," which provides the location, time, and general features of the major religious system detailed in the myths. A comprehensive index, titled "Names of the Goddess," provides all available names, with variants. Stories, rites, invocations, and prayers are recorded in the Myths section, as well as a list of common symbols. Never before has such a vast panorama of female divinity been recorded in one source.

1-56718-465-0, 384 pp., 8 $^1/_2$ x 11, illus., photos, softcover   **$19.95**

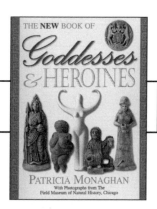

Magical Herbalism
The Secret Craft of the Wise
Scott Cunningham

Certain plants are prized for the special range of energies—the vibrations, or powers—they possess. Magical Herbalism unites the powers of plants and man to produce, and direct, change in accord with human will and desire.

This is the Magic of amulets and charms, sachets and herbal pillows, incenses and scented oils, simples and infusions and anointments. It's Magic as old as our knowledge of plants, an art that anyone can learn and practice, and once again enjoy as we look to the Earth to rediscover our roots and make inner connections with the world of Nature.

This is Magic that is beautiful and natural—a Craft of Hand and Mind merged with the Power and Glory of Nature: a special kind that does not use the medicinal powers of herbs, but rather the subtle vibrations and scents that touch the psychic centers and stir the astral field in which we live to work at the causal level behind the material world.

This is the Magic of Enchantment . . . of word and gesture to shape the images of mind and channel the energies of the herbs. It is a Magic for everyone—for the herbs are easily and readily obtained, the tools are familiar or easily made, and the technology that of home and garden. This book includes step-by-step guidance to the preparation of herbs and to their compounding in incense and oils, sachets and amulets, simples and infusions, with simple rituals and spells for every purpose.

0-87542-120-2, 260 pp., 5¼ x 8, illus., softcover   **$9.95**

To order call 1-800-THE MOON
Prices subject to change without notice.

Mother Nature's Herbal
Judith Griffin, Ph.D.

A Zuni American Indian swallows the juice of goldenrod flowers to ease his sore throat … an East Indian housewife uses the hot spices of curry to destroy parasites … an early American settler rubs fresh strawberry juice on her teeth to remove tartar. People throughout the centuries have enjoyed a special relationship with Nature and her many gifts. Now, with *Mother Nature's Herbal*, you can discover how to use a planet full of medicinal and culinary herbs through more than 200 recipes and tonics. Explore the cuisine, beauty secrets and folk remedies of China, the Mediterranean, South America, India, Africa and North America. The book will also teach you the specific uses of flower essences, chakra balancing, aromatherapy, essential oils, companion planting, organic gardening and theme garden designs.

1-56718-340-9, 448 pp., 7 x 10, color insert, softcover   **$19.95**

Mysteries of Isis
Her Worship & Magick
de Traci Regula

For 6,000 years, Isis has been worshiped as a powerful yet benevolent goddess who loves and cares for those who call on Her. Here, for the first time, Her secrets and mysteries are revealed in an easy-to-understand form so you can bring the power of this great and glorious goddess into your life.

Mysteries of Isis is filled with practical information on the modern practice of Isis' worship. Other books about Isis treat Her as an entirely Egyptian goddess, but this book reveals that she is a universal goddess with many faces, who has been present in all places and in all times. Simple yet effective rituals and exercises will show you how to forge your unique personal alliance with Isis: prepare for initiation into Her four key mysteries, divine the future using the Sacred Scarabs, perform purification and healing rites, celebrate Her holy days, travel to your own inner temple, cast love spells, create your own tools and amulets, and much more. Take Isis as your personal goddess and your worship and connection with the divine will be immeasurably enriched.

1-56178-560-6, 320 pp., 7 x 10, illus., softcover $19.95

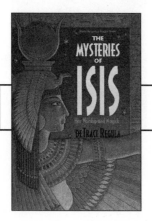

To order call 1-800-THE MOON
Prices subject to change without notice.